Wild Woodlands

WILD W

Photographs and Text by

BILL THOMAS

Taylor Publishing Company / Dallas, Texas

The Old-Growth Forests
of AMERICA

OODLANDS

Also by Bill Thomas

American Rivers: A Natural History
The Island
The Swamp
Talking with the Animals

Photograph on page 4 by Alan Lowell.
Underwater photographs on pages
31, 32-3, and 35 by Dan Richards.
Wildlife photographs on page 83 by John Ebeling.
Porcupine photograph on page 93 by Denny Dumas.

Published by Taylor Publishing Company
1550 West Mockingbird Lane
Dallas, Texas 75235

Designed by Whitehead and Whitehead

Library of Congress Cataloging-in-Publication Data

Thomas, Bill, 1934—
Wild woodlands: the old-growth forests of America/
photographs and text by Bill Thomas.
p. cm.
ISBN 0-87833-804-7
1. Forest ecology—United States. 2. Old growth
forests—United States. I. Title.
QH541.5.F6T52 1992
581.5'2642'0973—dc20   92-10979
CIP

Printed in the United States of America

10 9 8 7 6 5 4 3 2 1

This book is printed on acid-free recycled paper.

To the ancient Druids
and to all tree lovers
since

Contents

The Great Smokies.

The Forest:
A World of Its Own

The forest is a place of miracles, often filled with serenity and an unfathomable sense of peace. Nothing is so majestic nor filled with such genuine beauty as an old-growth forest, resplendent in any season of the year, nor so devastating and depressing as the clearcut demise of giant trees. A healthy behemoth woods is a source of endless fascination, for it embodies eternal mysteries and is home to more creatures than many other diverse ecosystems of our planet.

Humankind has been terribly busy slaying the forest for hundreds of years, stripping the land of the great trees which now are almost gone. But there still exists in pockets across the land remnants of what once was, reminding us of the vast woodlands stretching across much of this continent and others beyond. When we cut down the behemoth forest, we destroyed not only the big trees, but the god-creations of a thousand years, wiping aside the respect and admiration of the ages.

I live in remnants of an old-growth forest. There are no stumps left from where man sawed down the giants, no ax chips scattered upon the ground. A tiny winding road leads through the forest, shadowed by a canopy of great live oaks that curl 150 feet overhead, their limbs decorated with verdant growths of resurrection ferns and draped with silver tapestries of Spanish moss. The gently rolling land of this north Florida woodland is covered with cinnamon ferns, smilax, and a carpet of partridge berry. Holly trees make up a good deal of the understory. A mosaic of fallen timbers, some of which crashed to the floor as much as a century ago, hosts soft carpets of iridescent green moss.

During the warm weather months, the forest is host and home to swarms of insects, butterflies, red shoulder hawks, crows, wild hog, deer, wild turkey, and various kinds of snakes, including eastern diamondback rattlers, cottonmouth moccasins, coral and vine snakes, and tiny ringnecks. Colonies of great barred owls come calling at my house almost every day, swooping past my windows or peering in from some tree perch watching me work at the typewriter. They call incessantly, sometimes with a laughing sound, and sometimes during the wee hours of the night they awaken me to listen to their courtship.

In late winter, hordes of zebra butterflies, which normally are only found in the subtropics or tropics, flit through my old-growth woodland, alighting here and there to sample the pores of plants and the nectar of flowers. Sulphurs, fritillaries, and swallowtails play here, too. In the spring, millions of tiny frogs emerge, marching to the pond on the perimeter of my acreage. They are no longer than half an inch, and one must be terribly careful not to step on them.

Sometimes I have had to wait in my vehicle when driving out the driveway to allow a slider turtle to finish laying her eggs, or a snake to cross the road. But I am patient, for I know this is more their home than mine; besides, I find their activities far more fascinating than those in which I am so busily engaged.

From the pond (which some folks hereabouts call a lake) that sometimes drops dangerously low because of lack of rain, come the sounds on warm nights of small alligators, wood duck, great blue herons, and great egrets, punctuated with the calls of fussy greenback herons. Sometimes they can barely be heard above the overwhelming chorus of frogs which literally fills the air.

This pond, which covers some four to five acres, is called simply The Hog Pond. It was so named not because some farmer raised hogs there, but because it reportedly was created by the wallowings of wild hogs over hundreds of years. The wild hogs still occasionally come there; I see their signs more than I see them, and I imagine their wanderings this way are under cover of darkness. I am told by natives of this area that there are many Indian artifacts concealed in the black muck around the pond; one farmer told me that when he was a teenager he and his friends even dug up a hollow-log cypress canoe they believed might have been carved by Indians.

I'm firmly convinced that the pond and its creatures are strongly and unequivocally connected to the woodland. As I write this book, I am fortunately afforded a fantastic view of great oak trees, reminding me that they have stood silently here for half a millenium and that little more happened here yesterday than a century or two ago. There is—and surely has been all these years—drama of some sort every day: a bluejay plucking feathers from the back of one of the great owls, or a flight of crows zeroing in on a passing hawk.

One afternoon, as I lay upon the ground studying the activities of a small flock of finches darting from tree limb to tree limb in a light sprinkle of rain, I suddenly spotted a southern bald eagle soaring overhead. It passed by quickly, but I distinctly saw it cock its head slightly to look at me. Within a few minutes it returned, circled, and, unable to determine just what I was doing in a prone position on the forest floor, swooped downward. It came to rest on a bough of one of the great oaks. It sat there, peering at me with those piercing golden eyes until I moved to get a better look myself. Then it left as suddenly as it had come. It was the first and only eagle I have ever seen in my woods, although I'm sure over the centuries many have paused here from time to time.

It is indeed an awesome experience, living in these ancient woods. The pace of life is so very different than that outside the locked gate leading into my forest.

Old-growth Sitka spruce and Ponderosa pine, Olympic Peninsula, Washington.

Fir and spruce dominate at higher elevation in the Olympics. (photo by Alan Lowell)

Everything here seems poetically in place, each coming to rest in its particular niche over eons of time. There is a harmony in the scheme of life difficult to explain or understand unless... unless, of course, you have lived here, too, and have experienced it just as I have.

Only when we begin to perceive the totality of life that extends even beyond Planet Earth into the everlasting reaches of the universe can we begin to understand something about what we sometimes refer to as "the big picture," or the infinity of time and space. There is an ironic relativity about every form of life. My 400-year-old oak trees which appear ancient as I look upon them are mere infants in age compared to the 4000-year-old twisted bristlecone pines in the high deserts of California and Nevada. And how can I even comprehend the differences in size and growth between these great specimens and the mighty sequoia or redwood of California?

Old growth, of course, does not necessarily mean virgin forest, but virgin forest invariably means old growth. A virgin forest is one which has reached maturity through natural processes, technically speaking, and has not been influenced by human activity. Virgin forests theoretically do not exist today, simply because it's impossible to find, perhaps anywhere on earth, a forest that is not influenced by human society. Take pollution, for instance. Traces of carbon monoxide (automobile exhaust fumes) have been detected at both poles. Acid rain is another problem in

The Kenai River, southwest of Anchorage, Alaska.

Old logs on a beach tell a story: these may have been uprooted by windfall or an ocean storm.

many parts of the world. Old growth, of course, is largely determined by how long a forest has stood without harvesting the trees—any of the trees—and forests where dead trees and snags have been left standing until they fell of natural causes. Also, the logs and debris falling naturally upon the forest floor must have been left to decay naturally under the influence of natural elements.

It behooves us to define further just what old-growth forest really is, though it is, at best, a difficult and improbable task. While working on this book, I was told by foresters holding great expertise in such matters that groves of paperbark birch in the North Woods were old growth even though their girth near the base did not exceed three feet. It was a matter of lifespan; there on the scant soil of the Canadian Shield, a tree is lucky to reach 150 years of age before it experiences a natural death. The giant sequoias, comparatively speaking, have not yet reached teenage status at that point. Old growth, among those groves, exceeds 200 years and may reach up to 4,000, while the coastal redwoods attain only half that age.

In the southern piney woods, old growth may not exceed 200 years of age. In the desert southwest, the great saguaros are seldom more than 150 years of age. So old-growth parameters vary from place to place and from tree to tree. One thing is rather

Big Cypress Swamp, Florida.

certain: wherever you encounter old-growth or ancient trees, you'll immediately recognize them. There is a certain atmosphere about an old-growth forest that distinctly sets it apart. You can feel the years, the sanctity of its very being. If you enter alone, you likely will walk silently, often with mouth agape. If you accompany another, you'll soon find yourself communicating in hand signals or speaking in hushed tones or whispers, almost as though anything more is sacrilegious.

The respect for age in the community of humankind also, I think, occurs in communities of other species, if not in all forms of life. Frequently, I go for long early-morning walks in my own woods. Seldom do I pass up the matriarchs without pausing to gaze upon them, to scan the height of their structure, to gingerly touch the bark that girds their mighty trunks.

Old-growth trees provide a viable link between the past, present, and future. They have lived through generations of humans; in some cases they have even witnessed the birth, life, and death of entire cultures. Many of the trees who have become my daily companions have experienced, in most cases, all types of hazards, storms, plagues, diseases, and damaging insects such as the gypsy moth, and yet somehow still stand.

Okefenokee alligator.

When Leif Ericson's fleet was cutting old-growth trees from the shores of North America to supply building needs in Greenland, long before Columbus came to this hemisphere, the forests were already old, spanning thousands of years—millenium. The stories they tell are far more important accounts of nature's transcendance than the puny creations of man. Because of their age and because they are conceived by the natural elements of the universe, they are of special importance.

By now, most of us realize that nothing in nature stands alone. We can only guarantee the longevity of ancient forests through our careful study and understanding of biodiversity. Every element of our world is strongly intertwined and connected, like the fine strands of a spider's web. We must not only understand that, but agree and support its every premise in all that we do. The harmony afforded by such relationships is an important proponent of the very fiber of life. Without it, the quality and length of our life is greatly reduced.

Yet every now and then an individual or group of individuals rises to a position of influence in our society who would eliminate the great trees. Secretary of the Interior James Watt, holding office during the early years of the Reagan administration, in 1981 suggested selling lands contained in the national parks and wilderness areas in order to help decrease the national deficit. About that same time Ronald Reagan tried to blame trees as among the worst polluters of the land. Greedy timber barons ravage the Amazon rainforests at devastating rates and no one dares stand in their way. In 1988, rubber tapper and activist Francisco "Chico" Mendez was assassinated while trying to protect that rainforest from developers. All of us are somewhat guilty of taking trees for granted. No one, for instance, is ever so aware of how much a tree means to his or her feeling of well-being until it is felled—land, sky, and mind suddenly laid bare.

An ancient inhabitant of the Great Smokies.

Above. *A bobcat deep in the woods of the Heartlands.*
Left. *Paperback birch in the Boundary Waters area along the Minnesota-Canadian border.*

The European nations, being more cognizant of diminishing resources simply because their civilizations are older, are now fully aware of the value of forests. No clearcutting is allowed anywhere on the continent. Switzerland was the first to ban it; Germany has long had laws against clearcutting and foresters there are working on a sustainable forest which ideally will last forever. One German forester told me, "We are now so much more aware of all the interrelationships that exist in a forest. If we do not do our job of adequate management, we may destroy countless other communities of creatures, thereby depleting, perhaps forever, vital links in the chain of life."

He is, of course, absolutely correct. All too often, we think only of the trees, not of the other dependent life forms strongly tied to the life of trees. Germany, for instance, only a few centuries ago was literally covered with old-growth forest; today it is reduced to plantation (managed) forests. "Sentimentality," said one veteran German forester, "should be the heart of the forest." Without ethical values, something is wrong in our appreciation of woods—and life.

There are, of course, more of old-forest ecosystems on the planet than we record. Some are too small to be noted, smaller even than the virgin red spruce stand in the Unaka Mountains of eastern Tennessee's Cherokee National Forest. Bob Eaton, silvaculturist on the Cherokee, describes this particular tract as a bowl surrounded by steep ridges that have protected it both against logging and the terrible 1925 fire that destroyed much of the woodlands around it. Some of the red spruce, he says, are close to four feet in diameter at the base. Once there were seas of red spruce all the way to Maine and beyond into Canada's Maritimes, many flourishing into the early part of this century, but today they are almost all gone.

While there are no large stands of old growth noted in the Rockies, either, there are a few smaller ones of Ponderosa pine in various national forests. Hundreds of acres of old-growth forest are privately owned throughout America; probably no state is without one or more such tracts. But since they are privately controlled, their future is questionable. While the present owners may have the preservation of the forest at heart, they cannot provide any guarantees as to what will happen to it after their own demise.

Owners of old-growth forest need to take note of one landmark case which actually occurred a few years ago just outside Washington, D.C. It involves an aged bachelor, Seton Belt, who owned a farm on which stood an impressive tract of old-growth forest. Many of the trees dated back beyond the discovery of this continent by Christopher Columbus. Seton Belt loved his forest and when he died in 1959, he left his farm including the old-growth forest to St. Barnabas Episcopal Church.

Belt clearly stated in his will that the trustees of his estate, the Mercantile Safe-Deposit and Trust Company, of Baltimore, expressly prohibit and enjoin from selling any part of his farm; the woods were not to be cut but "used only for the purpose of repairs and improvements to the buildings and fences and for firewood."

For years both the church and the trustees sought ways to make money from the land. In 1980, after a few branches had damaged cars parked at adjoining Tall Oaks School in Maryland, they decided the old-growth forest was past mature and ought to be harvested. They succeeded in changing the will and, shortly thereafter, huge trees, some of them more than 300 years old, began crashing to the ground. Even though he had generously given the church a monument it could never have had otherwise, Seton Belt's wishes obviously meant nothing. The only part of the woods now protected is a small portion purchased during the eleventh hour by the state of Maryland, which set it aside as a state park. The cut-over portion is now being developed by the church as a moneymaking real estate subdivision.

Where one finds the old-growth forest, however, is somewhat immaterial. It holds the wisdom of centuries past, coupling the present and future. It provides the aesthetic values we, as human beings, desperately need for our own peace of mind, indeed our own sanity. A mushroom sprouting after a summer's rain speaks of the multiplicity of forms waiting only for the proper warmth and moisture to encourage them to emerge and scatter spores of seeds. A colorful broadleaf in autumn is more than just a gorgeous color against the sky; it is the story of the entire year—nature's growth and harvest and now, the prelude of death and decay as the forest heralds a new season—winter, the final one of the year. But even in the dead of winter, there is still life and meaning in the forest. A wing mark of a bird or a track on the winter's snow is evidence that though the coldest time of year has come, life goes on.

We are a nation in a hurry; our society rushes to keep pace with the endless treadmill that rushes madly on and results in no more than just more rushing. In attempting to keep that pace, we are afforded, as individuals, little time to appreciate the things of value around us. One of them, of course, is the woods. Robert Frost years ago tried to call our attention to it in his poem "Stopping by Woods on a Snowy Evening." There is no longer any time in our lives to stop by woods on a snowy evening, or any other evening.

The majority of our population is urban these days. People who live in cities adore trees, of course, even forests. They brighten up at the sight of a street with even the scrawniest sapling contradicting the concrete canyons in which they live. The pleasure of trees seems to root in us from the start of our lives, perhaps because as horizontal babies, a tree's branches were among the first prizes for which we reached. But the majority of us never really get to experience a woods, much less an old-growth forest.

Even once experienced, we so often do not see. I have for some years taught a series of nature photographic workshops in various parts of the nation and one of my greatest challenges is to make people aware, to encourage them not only to look, but to see. All too often they pass over the most interesting and unusual subjects, sometimes unknowingly stepping upon them.

During the late winter, when new life stirs within the bosom of the earth and on into the early warm days of spring, as whole communities of plants and flowers eagerly emerge, the woods take on new meaning. Distinct aromas fill the air as balmy southern breezes carry the sounds of thousands of birds winging their way northward. They fill the woods, looking for nest sites, each staking out territories for its own, dedicated to raising new families. The whir of insects punctuates the air.

The winter woods have been largely silent, but now the forest becomes busier than at any other time of year. An anxiety prevails; so much is to be done, as summer is on the threshold and fall is soon to follow. Life is awakening; movement and change are in the air. The woods during the winter belong to sleeping creatures, or to those doing little more than housekeeping chores. But not any more. Life in the spring woods becomes vibrant and directed. Secrets that have been concealed all winter in the woods now are uncovered and shared.

Snowy owl near Hudson Bay.

A stand of old cottonwood in New Mexico.

Even the most minute plant life seems in a hurry. Tiny British soldiers spring from the mosses on dead logs, their red hats beaming in the sun. Fiddlehead ferns break the crust of the earth under a blanket of needles or leaves, pushing their way upward, searching for the warmth of the sun. In pools of water collected from winter snowmelt or spring rains an aquatic community begins to function and interact, like some miracle created by the gods. Occasionally I pause to peer into the mirrored pools, hoping to observe and resolve some of the mystery that goes on there. Sometimes I see nothing but a reflection of myself; sometimes of the big lazy cumulus clouds floating in the skies above me. But every so often I am fortunate enough to witness a mosquito larvae jerking and wriggling to the surface for air, a caddis worm climbing sedately up a stem with its back-borne camouflage of tiny bits of grass and grains of sand, a diving beetle with a tail-held silver bubble, a newly hatched tadpole scurrying over the mud. Here in a single tiny puddle on the forest floor is the microcosm of life's creation.

Even as this miracle occurs beneath my feet, zillions of others are also in the process throughout the woodland. Bursting buds on every twig of every hardwood tree herald the coming of spring; if they each could play a trumpet, the whole universe would hear. It is a time of great celebration; so exciting is the event I am somewhat surprised I can tear myself away from it even long enough to find food to sustain me. The magic that occurs in any forest, old-growth or otherwise, during the springtime is indeed one of the most fascinating happenings on the planet.

One springtime I attended a survival school which taught, among other things, measures to sharpen one's alertness to the immediate surroundings. One of those exercises was to lie face down on the woodland floor, with head lifted just a couple of inches. We were to lie there for two hours, shutting out all else around us except one single square foot of space.

At first, we saw very little in our tiny world reduced to a single square foot. But the longer we looked, the more we saw. Creatures we did not even realize were there soon began to move about, resuming their housekeeping chores and other activities, having gained confidence we were not there to cause them harm. A tiny ladybug, often found in forests these days, but an exotic introduced not so many years ago from another land, began to explore its immediate environment. A tiny inch worm measured off the height of a blade of grass. A pixie red ant crawled past the inch worm, stopping every few steps to look upward as though to ascertain its own safety. Dwarflike plants and mosses and lichens I hadn't even noticed soon became major components of my new world.

Soon I began not only to notice things I saw, but sounds and smells and even the things I felt. A spider no larger than a pinhead began stringing a web under my very nose. For a moment, I thought it was going to attach it to a hair in one nostril. Had I not moved, it might have, and my nose would have become a full participant in this new network, perhaps trapping flying insects for the little spider's lunch. Thoughts began to flow more freely in my mind, thoughts I had never entertained before. Now I became aware of what was really happening; I was becoming, bit by bit, an integral part of the forest. The tiny microcosm unfolding before me, inches away from my face, was integrating itself into the very fiber of my spirit just as I was becoming a part of this small parcel of Mother Earth. I began to feel a oneness. True, no trees grew here, but they were all around me. I could feel their presence. I could hear the zephyrs whisper through them, could feel the breeze stir the hair on my bare arms.

This was a fine lesson in sensitivity. Through this simple exercise, I not only was becoming more aware, but I realized the universe was limitless, that it truly extended on and on and on into infinity. And I began more fully to realize, too, that what really was most important was this square foot of land. If I really knew and understood this tiny piece of real estate, I could more fully know all the other square feet of real estate on the entire planet.

The act of finally realizing my relationship to the forest and its to me was so exuberating I felt adrenalin pumping, my heart drumming to a new song. There was newfound peace surging through me, though I understood the forest was still—and always would be—a mystery.

Among other things, I knew I didn't fully realize the chemical reactions going on that would support new life, even my own. Seldom considered but of vital importance is the release of carbon. Plants, through photosynthesis, convert carbon dioxide to carbohydrates and can thus store carbon within their tissue.

This storage of carbon is only temporary, as vegetation ultimately releases carbon back into the atmosphere through decomposition. Forest vegetation accounts for approximately 90 percent of the vast amounts of carbon stored in the biomass of terrestrial ecosystems. Forty percent is currently contained within the temperate and boreal regions of the world. The remainder is concentrated primarily in tropical forests, which typically have a greater average biomass and can thus store greater amounts of carbon.

Since the early 1800s, the ever-increasing use of fossil fuels has liberated increasing quantities of carbon dioxide. The world's oceans and diminished forests simply cannot provide an endless sink for this carbon; consequently, about one half the carbon dioxide gas produced each year from human activities now accumulates in the atmosphere. Within the next fifty years, considering today's rate of use of fossil fuels, the amount of carbon dioxide in the atmosphere could very well double.

Because of this, scientists are now predicting that global temperatures may rise as much as two degrees centigrade within the next half century or less. The result could include the melt-down of glaciers and the polar ice caps, thus dramatically raising the levels of the oceans, plus drastic shifts in the climatically suitable agriculture zones. The changes in carbon could substantially affect the productivity of many plants, including domestic food plants, resulting in great famine over many parts of the globe.

Deforested areas, besides not being able to absorb carbon, also become producers of it in their own right. Land clearance in the tropics, for example, which is proceeding at an estimated rate of one percent of the total land area of the world every year, may contribute half again as much carbon dioxide as is released by fossil fuels. Therefore the preservation of all possible reservoirs, or sinks, of carbon has become critical. Detailed studies of the world's temperate forests, to identify areas where intensive forest management can enhance carbon accumulation in the future, may prove not only of great value, but of paramount importance in our own survival.

Today less than 25 percent of North America is in woodland and only one-tenth of one percent in primeval condition. When we think of the diminishing biomass it is indeed frightening how close to annihilation we now live.

If, for instance, we consider our present dilemma in terms of chemical analysis, we simply must consider the amount of biomass provided by the Amazonian rainforest, the temperate rainforest of the Olympic Peninsula, western Canada, and southeast Alaska, and one other site seldom mentioned, the lower Mississippi River Valley.

The Mississippi's rich bottomlands not so many years ago were dense old-growth woodlands of tupelo gum and bald cypress, but today virtually all of this area has been cleared for croplands—cotton and soybeans. The United States Forest Service estimates that at current rates of conversion, the bottomlands of the entire Southeast will be drained, deforested, and planted in crops by 1995. Logging, however, has not been the only problem over the years. Blights, insects, and fires have contributed to the demise of the forests as well. The American chestnut, devastated by blight in the early 1900s, was once a dominant species in the southern Appala-

Saguaro National Monument, Arizona.

Methuselah trees—the great sequoias.

chians. The present forest of smaller trees provides far less biomass and can therefore store less carbon.

The great forest has many redeeming qualities important to our lives. Walk into the woods on the hottest day and you'll immediately notice the change in temperature. Think of the role a dense forest canopy plays in creating a healthy forest environment, not to mention global climate.

For millions of years forests have played an important ecological role in the checks and balances of nature. As long as that balance is maintained, the world is a beautiful and healthy place. But in the face of imbalance, everything in nature becomes a potential problem area. The beauty and the balance are connected, and they are what sustains us.

This is the forest primeval. The murmuring
  pines and the hemlocks,
Bearded with moss, and in garments green,
  indistinct in the twilight,
Stand like Druids of eld, with voices sad and
  prophetic,
Stand like harpers hoar, with beards that rest
  on their bosoms.
Loud from its rocky caverns, the deep-voiced
  neighboring ocean
Speaks, and in accents disconsolate answers the
  wail of the forest.

Henry Wadsworth Longfellow, *Evangeline*

Sunset in the 10,000 Islands at Rookery Bay.

ONE

Forests of the Sea

The most improbable old-growth forests on Planet Earth seem almost a novelty; they are the forests of the sea. Broadly stated, they include two basic types—the mangrove forests, which grow on stilts and flirt with the ocean's tides, and the other forest, underwater, the kelp forest, swaying with the waves just as forests above water sway in the breezes of the wind. Each is distinctly different in many ways from the other, but each shares many qualities with more commonly known old-growth forests.

There are three different types of mangrove—red, black, and white—and in North America it is found only in semitropical areas. It grows profusely in many other parts of the world: New Zealand, Australia, the islands of the South Pacific, Central and South America. But in North America, it is found only in south Florida. Once it ventured north of Tampa Bay on the Gulf Coast for more than fifty years, but one cold winter in the 1970s put an end to it. Today the old-growth mangrove is confined mainly to the Florida Keys, the islands of Florida Bay, and the Ten Thousand Islands of southwest Florida.

While the kelp forest, which is wholly contained within the oceans, grows in many parts of the marine world, one of the principal forests within the United States is found around the Channel Islands off southern California and particularly on the north end of Santa Barbara Island. Here it grows to remarkable heights—100 feet or more tall. Some people consider it seaweed, but it is more commonly known as a forest. And when you explore it yourself, there is no question: it's a forest, with trees that sway as though responding to a fine orchestra. Fishes of all descriptions glide among the branches like birds flitting from tree limb to tree limb in conventional land-locked forests.

I became acquainted with these two forests about the same time. I lived for a short period in the Florida Keys while working on a book called *The Island* back in the mid-1970s. Later in that same decade, I camped on Anacapa and Santa Barbara islands in the Channel Isles while working on the same book. My adventures in the kelp forest were comparatively brief, although I did get a good feel for what it was like. But during 1974–76, I spent a great deal of time exploring the mangrove forests of the Florida Keys and the mangrove islands that make up the archipelago called the Ten Thousand Islands south of Naples on the Gulf.

Much of this area in Florida originated since the Pleistocene geologic period (some two million years ago) and most of it since the last great Ice Age (about ten thousand years ago). While no glaciers reached this far south, they certainly had an effect upon the land. With so much water being frozen in the glaciers, the sea level was substantially lower, thus providing greater areas for the propagation of the mangrove forest. In fact, if you were to lower the sea level just ten feet, the size of the Florida peninsula would be nearly double its present size. Most of the area in what is commonly known as the Continental Shelf would have been above water during the Ice Age, and even greater amounts of it if the oceans were lowered ten feet.

On the other hand, if the ocean levels were raised ten feet, about half of the present state of Florida would disappear. Remarkable, isn't it? Roughly, that much area south of Florida Bay is where one finds mangrove growing today, along the brackish waterways leading from the sea. Mangroves will grow in saltwater, of course, but they seem to prefer brackish water best—that is, water diluted by some freshwater.

While mangrove do not have a reputation of being old anywhere in the world, there are some scientists who believe they may reach seventy-five to one hundred years of age in the Ten Thousand Islands area, as well as in some portions of the Keys. Many are ripped from their moorings by ocean storms, of course, short of the century mark. But, by the same token this is part of the role they play in protecting the land. For years, the U.S. Corps of Engineers was guilty of either destroying mangrove or allowing permits for developers to destroy it. That came to an end when the mangrove was finally recognized in the sixties and seventies as the greatest natural deterrent against hurricane damage.

My first encounter with mangrove was in the early 1960s when I was working as travel editor of a large Midwest metropolitan newspaper. I took a tour of south Florida and the Keys. Renting a convertible in Miami, I drove the 126-mile length of the Keys one moonlit night in November. It was marvelous. Some of the road was bounded by mangrove, forming a dark vinelike jungle. Later on the same trip, I visited John Pennekamp State Park on Key Largo and discovered mangrove closer up. So massive were they that, it was easy to understand why they presented a barrier against tropical storms.

On that same trip, I freelanced a fishing story for one of the outdoor magazines in New York. Two locals—Conchs, they are called, if a native of the Keys—took me aboard their boat out of Sugarloaf Key some thirty five miles from Key West. They told me a remarkable thing about the many islands of Florida Bay—they said they had actually seen mangrove islands born during their lifetime. "Sometimes," one of them told me, "severe ocean storms would tear an island from its moorings—

Above. *Older mangrove, forming
a community which will soon
begin building new land.*
Right. *Liguus tree snails, which
come in more than forty color
combinations, are found in many
of the old-growth mangrove
islands, but attached to other
types of smooth-bark trees.*

Above. *A great white heron, found in most of the mangrove islands.*
Left. *A maze of red mangrove roots.*

Above. *Osprey, an endangered species also known as the fish hawk, nest in the mangrove islands.*
Right. *Old-growth mangrove.*

Above. *Small sprigs of mangrove on a mudflat soon will begin building a new island.*
Left. *Raccoon on Sanibel Island, much of which consists of old-growth mangrove.*

Tiny Key deer, hardly larger than a German shepherd dog, inhabit several of the mangrove islands of the lower Florida Keys.

mangrove roots—and the island might drift for several days before touching bottom again, where the mangrove roots would quickly anchor it to the sea floor once more."

"I'll bet it would be really startling to be anchored in your boat fishing and have an island smack you from behind," I replied, half believing their story. But later on, and upon a number of occasions, I heard that story repeated in other parts of the Keys by other old Conchs until I finally believed it to be true. I daresay it doesn't happen often, but I now believe it does happen.

The mangrove are unbelievable in their role for creating new land. The red mangrove, for example, miraculously creates its own forest from the sea. First, ocean currents and tiny coral animals build a reef, sandbar, or mudflat, vulnerable to tides and storms. Few plants can gain a foothold, for not many are saltwater tolerant. But the red mangrove seed, which looks somewhat like a large green bean, drops from the parent tree into the ocean. It floats upright with most of the lower half submerged. When the end of it touches the floor of the shallow sea, it almost immediately puts forth a holdfast and roots into the soil. This holds the seed steady while stronger roots protrude, confirming the anchor. Within a few days, the other end of the seed has produced a small plant with leaves, and a mangrove tree is born.

Within a year, it has grown large enough to put out "feeler" roots above the surface of the water. It then looks like a great spider, clutching the bottom like gnarled fingers. The struggle for survival is powerful indeed, and as soon as the tangled root network forms, the ocean currents begin bringing driftwood, debris, and decaying sea life which the roots catch. Larger and larger the pile of debris becomes until it decays and forms humus, creating the base for other life—marine creatures, insects, other plants. A sandy, mucky soil forms, and the mangrove then sends up unique breathing roots that emerge from the mud like shaving-brush bristles.

Other seedling mangroves soon form a whole community, and the island-building process is repeated over and over again. Within a few years, the accumulation of debris and humus around each mangrove tree connects, one with another, and an island is born. A few years ago, I did an article for *Sierra* magazine and subsequently another one for *Oceans* magazine on that very subject. One of them pointed out Florida Bay as the place where islands are born. They still are and will continue to be for a long time to come.

The mangrove has three kinds of roots. One is normal roots—the ones the mangrove puts down first that anchor it into the floor of the ocean. The second is the prop root, stabilizing it against ocean waves and storms that might topple it over. The third is the aerial root or air-breather, which comes up from the underground roots for the purpose of providing oxygen.

Wherever there are mudflats or coral reefs in the tropics or subtropics, you'll likely find this remarkable process underway—the creation of new land. And all three types of roots play an important role. Although not so fast that the eye can see it happen in one viewing, the mind and memory can if you are in close contact with the islands in these areas.

In the Ten Thousand Islands are what scientists believe to be the oldest growth of mangrove forests. Although there are older islands that support other kinds of tree life in this area, most of the Ten Thousand Islands are mangrove islands. Actually, there may be more than 10,000 of them. No one really knows, for the islands are always changing, some splitting away and becoming satellite islands during a single ocean storm. New ones are constantly being born. And in the deeper regions of the islands, some only separated from each other by narrow estuaries which serve as incubators for multitudes of marine life, are found large red mangrove with prop roots as high as one's head. At high tide, they stand in water; at low tide the ocean runs away, leaving a mucky wet soil with a most active community of creatures—sea worms, crabs, snails, mangrove periwinkles, mollusks, and millions of other forms of life. They hurry about housekeeping or catching food, obviously engaged in all kinds of chores during the brief time each day before the ocean tide returns and their homes are underwater again.

I used to paddle my canoe into some of these areas, waiting for low tide so I could just sit and listen to the bustle of life around me. There were songs, whistles, and squeaky sounds the likes of which I had never heard before or since. And all kinds of oceangoing life comes here, too, even sharks, as well as a number of saltwater fish and endangered manatee, all cruising the estuaries. The Ten Thousand Islands is perhaps one of the most important places in this hemisphere contributing to the propagation of oceangoing marine life. And the mangrove is the catalyst that makes it all happen.

One must have a special understanding and affection for mangrove to appreciate them. They've never been very popular with society at large. Growing mostly in humid conditions, they too often have been associated, erroneously in most cases, with pestilence and disease. Old wives' tales describe them as dense tangles of aerial roots which harbor not only mosquitoes, gnats that are all jaws, crocodiles (and there are some in the upper Keys and in the Ten Thousand Islands as well—the only ones found in the wild in North America), but also snakes and unspeakable parasites. One Conch storyteller tried to convince me that the AIDS virus actually originated in the mangrove swamps.

Above. *The 10,000 Islands area of southwest Florida from 600 feet up.*
Right. *Roseate spoonbills, which get their brilliant color from their saltwater diet, feed on the mudflats surrounding mangrove islands.*

Above. *At low tide in the 10,000 Islands, the mangrove stands above the water in black muck; at high tide it may be under three feet of water.*
Left. *A yellow-crown night heron.*

In spite of these common (or uncommon) misconceptions, the mangrove has long been a subject of admiration and wonder. Theophrastus, a student of Aristotle, wrote the first botanical description of mangroves, observing that they have their roots always flooded by the sea and, nevertheless, the tree does not perish. Novelist John Steinbeck, best known for his Pulitzer-Prize-winning *The Grapes of Wrath* and that lovable little book, *Travels with Charley,* wrote in *The Log of the Sea of Cortez,* "Nobody likes the mangroves. Their foul odor and the impenetrable quality of their roots . . . gives one a feeling of dislike for these salt-water eating bushes."

The foul odor, of course, does not come from the mangroves, but from sulphur deposits from decaying marine matter. Not always is it found with mangrove, but most usually in areas where water is trapped in pools and becomes stagnant.

The mangroves particularly are incubators and protectors for early fish life. Many species of fish are quite vulnerable when young. Clustered within the roots' protection, huge shimmering schools of fry can be seen; when trouble approaches they dart back into the confines of the root maze. In Florida, for example, 90 percent of all commercial fish spend part of their life cycle in mangrove-lined estuaries. The Florida shrimp and spiny lobster are heavily dependent upon the health of the mangroves.

Ecologist William Odum of the University of Virginia's Department of Environmental Sciences says another valuable contribution of mangroves is the food they provide. Technically evergreen, the mangrove seeds the waters at its feet every day of the year, for it is constantly shedding. Odum says a one-acre stand of red mangrove may produce as many as three tons of leaves during a single year. Bacteria and plankton feast constantly on the leaves and thereby begins the food chain, for they are then consumed by small fish, which in turn, are food for larger fish.

The red mangrove normally is the source tree for all this creative process (the building of land mass and islands) and a healthy marine environment. As new generations of red mangroves move outward from a land mass, another species, the black mangrove, begins to take hold in the island's vacated center, which by now is no more than a foot above sea level. This process continues. Other plants such as sea grape and white mangrove also appear and add to the structure of the island and to its diversity of plants.

Among the first creatures to arrive and play a role in this island-building process are barnacles, sponges, and oysters. Wading birds such as great blue herons, white herons, egrets, greenback herons, and reddish egrets come, too, and soon creatures such as raccoons show up. The accumulated silt attracts the larvae of burrowing worms, shrimp, and clams, which soon begin to establish booming populations. Fiddler crabs, snails, and insects swarm to this virgin territory.

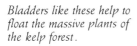

Bladders like these help to float the massive plants of the kelp forest.

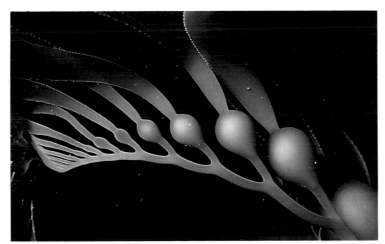

Opaleye and black surfperch in the kelp
forest off the California coast.

Long before there was man, the mangrove forest was doing exactly what it's doing today—creating new land mass. It likely will be doing so long after man disappears from the planet as well. So will the forest lying just under the sea—kelp. Although kelp forests do occur in various places of the ocean, I have chosen one of the most accessible ones off the California coast simply because it is handy and easily studied.

Attached to the rocky substratum by a conical, rootlike holdfast, the kelp (*Macrocystis*) reaches up to the light above, often spreading its leaves on the surface to form a dense canopy. The stemlike stipes are buoyed by gas-filled bladders from which grow long, leafy fronds. Nutrients in the water are synthesized with energy from the sun and passed down to nourish the rest of the plant in its twilight world below.

Divers who have experienced the kelp forest often describe the play of light which escapes in well-defined shafts through the canopy as "cosmic." "It's like a kaleidoscope of subtle changes and patterns," one diver told me. "It's almost sur-realistic and beyond anything one could encounter in this world."

Plenty of wildlife exists in the kelp forest as well. It's a favorite lounging place for sea otter, masking crab (which is so adept at camouflage you may never see it even though you're looking directly at it), masses of red and yellow sponges, the multi-hued sabellid, feather-duster worm, and a greater array of anemones than you ever imagined could exist in one place. Sea slugs are everywhere, and there's an abun-dance of fish, some spending most of their life there to take advantage of the additional security offered by the forest. Sea cucumbers, sea urchins, and sea stars are abundant. In fact, one of the primary enemies of the kelp forest is the sea urchin, which feeds on the holdfasts. Once they have eaten through the holdfast, the kelp stipe is released and its bladders elevate it to the surface, where waves and currents carry it away. It is likely a sea urchin that contributes to the kelp debris you see on the beach.

So, in some ways the kelp forest is similar to the mangrove in that it provides a safer haven for many creatures of the sea. Without it, the survival rate of much of the marine life would be radically different. Sharks are frequent visitors to the kelp forest, but usually only to pass through out of curiosity. Occasionally seals and sea lions playfully dash in and out of the "trees" of the kelp forest as well. Fickle winds and currents sometimes carry jellyfish by the thousands into the forest, where they sometimes remain for days until the violent elements have subsided.

Quite often, salps in the forest are mistaken for jellyfish. They do look very similar. Their clear, hollow bodies and bioluminescent organs are most remarkable when they link together, side by side, to form long, beautiful chains. At the base of each animal is a yellow-orange organ which clearly stands out against the blue-green seawater. Otherwise, the bodies are transparent.

Even though considerable scientific study has been done over long periods of time on both the kelp forest and the mangrove forest, scientists readily admit that much is yet to be learned about both of these unusual environments. Indeed, it may be centuries, if ever, before all the secrets of these places are unlocked. I seriously doubt they'll discover what my old Conch friend believes—that AIDS started here in the mangroves. But, perhaps more realistically, they'll find a cure for it here. Who knows?

Above. *This plant shows the tentacle holdfast that anchors it to the floor of the sea.*
Below. *Growing almost 100 feet tall from the floor of the sea, the component parts of the kelp forest create a strange aura underwater, waving in the currents like trees above water sway in the wind.*

TWO

The Swamp Forest

t was dawn on a balmy April morning on the edge of South Carolina's sandhills when I slipped into one of America's most impressive old-growth forests. It was my first visit with the great behemoth trees of the awesome Congaree Swamp, which extends along the muddy river bottoms of a stream by the same name. The boundary was well marked with bold-lettered signs warning any intruder of the possibility of being shot with high-powered rifles. I was clearly a trespasser and was distinctly aware that I might be brought down by a bullet before the morning was finished.

Three others accompanied me on this mission to explore the swamp: John Dennis, the respected ornithologist from Massachusetts, who had, in fact, been in these woods two years previously, and two young interns from the South Carolina Department of Natural Resources who had been assigned to learn as much as they could about the innards of the swamp.

The Congaree Swamp was privately owned and off-limits to trespassers, especially back then in 1974. The Swamp had become a center of controversy. Environmental groups throughout the state and particularly in Columbia, the state capital, led by the efforts of the Sierra Club, were trying to save the Congaree—to achieve a takeover by the National Park Service which would lead to its status as a national monument.

This was my very first trip into the Congaree. What I found there was like discovering a little bit of America left untouched by the march of civilization. Time stood still. It was unbelievably quiet, except for the call of a Carolina wren or the far-off yammer of a great woodpecker.

"Ivory-bill," grinned Dennis from the forest shadows. When I chuckled in disbelief, he assured me that if indeed the ivory-bill did still exist anywhere, it probably would be found here. I spent the rest of the day scanning the woods above

37

Opposite. *A heron in the Big Cypress Swamp.*

Top. *A mother gator takes her young for a swim in the Florida Big Cypress.*
Left. *White ibis (the Indians call them curlews) gather to roost in spring in the Okefenokee.*
Above. *A Florida panther.*

A greenback heron.

me in hopes of being the first one to spot the ever-so-rare-if-not-extinct bird, which I had seen only in *Audubon* magazine. Giant trees stood all around us, some wading in muddy pools of unknown depth left by the spring floods during the past month. There was a prevailing air of longevity and peacefulness I had rarely encountered anywhere.

Of all the wild woodlands of the eastern United States, none are more lush nor possess greater elegance than the patriarch swamp forests south of the 40th parallel. Although only traces of this wholesome ecological system remain untouched, the swamp forest continues to be a vital and unique element in the role of a primeval woodland.

The swamp forest has long had significant geological impact upon the earth. During the greening period of the continent just following the great Devonian Age, lush swamps left a legacy, coal, which underlies all but a few of the United States and some of Canada. In the Carboniferous period, invertebrates flourished on land in shark-prowled waters. (The petroleum industry has relied upon the tiny marine animals of this time—single-celled protozoans with shells resembling wheat grains in size and shape—as index fossils for potential oil deposits.) The trees in the arboniferous swamps were somewhat different from those we find today. They were huge spore-bearing species related to the tiny club mosses of today, and there were giant horsetails and scale trees more than a hundred feet tall, with trunks six feet in diameter. The first winged insects coursed these forests, and amphibians, newly evolved from lobe-finned fishes, ventured ashore.

At one time the great swamp forests of our own geological age covered millions of acres along the waterways of the southeastern and southern portions of this continent. Between were upland and sandhill forests, but none compared with the unbroken canopies, the dense dank morass where stood giant monuments to America's wetlands. Virtually all of them have vanished before the saw and ax; now only sporadic instances of virgin swamp forest occur. Perhaps the most outstanding examples of swamp forest are found in the Four Holes and Congaree swamps of South Carolina, along the Neches River corridor of the Texas Big Thicket, and small portions of the Fakahatchee Strand of Florida's Big Cypress.

All of these were on the verge of annihilation when they were set aside during the eleventh hour of their existence to be preserved for posterity. But Congress only acted in part measure for the demands of environmentalist groups; in the Congaree and Big Thicket very limited acreage has been entrusted to protection and preservation for future generations. It took years of relentless effort before the voices of concerned citizens were heard, despite the fact that chain saws were eating away constantly at the forest. The Big Thicket, which once covered a vast portion of east Texas so dense it presented a formidable green barrier to all those who came that way, was almost no more by the time the encroachments of humanity were curtailed. And the Congaree Swamp forest, which contained numerous state and national record trees, might have been wiped from the face of the earth within another decade.

The Congaree Swamp forest was set aside in late 1976 as a national monument, to be administered by the National Park Service. Two years earlier, the Big Thicket had been set aside by the Department of the Interior as a national preserve, and the National Audubon Society and The Nature Conservancy purchased some 1800 acres

Eastern diamondback rattlers.

*Yellow-crown night heron
in the Texas Big Thicket.*

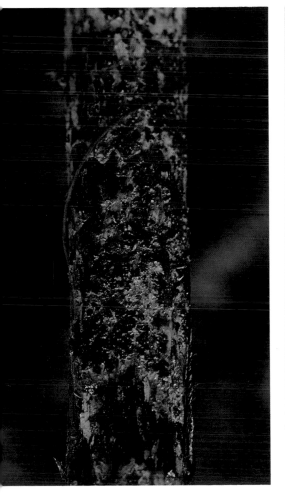

Left. *Baton rouge lichen.*
Above. *Pearl water lilies in the Okefenokee.*

Left. *Woods Bay, South Carolina.*
Below. *The Okefenokee.*

of the virgin Francis Beidler Memorial Forest in the Four Holes Swamp as a sanctuary. A few small tracts of virgin woods remain in the Okefenokee Swamp and in a few other scattered swamps throughout the South, including Florida's Big Cypress.

One of the most accessible old-growth swamp forests is the Fakahatchee Strand, where the state of Florida has built an elevated boardwalk for nearly half a mile. Except for hoards of feisty black mosquitos who live there most of the year, it is a veritable paradise. Without the mosquitos, of course, the forest would in time become something far less than paradise in many ways, since they're a vital factor in the natural food chain.

So impressive is this bit of virgin swampland forest that I take students from across America and around the world there with me for a major portion of a nature photographic workshop each year. I do so to introduce them to this unique environmental ecosystem only an hour's drive west of Miami in the low country of south Florida. During the first workshop I conducted there, a pair of bald eagles perched on a high loft extending from one of the huge cypresses directly over the boardwalk. Most of my students had never seen a bald eagle in the wild; now there were two just above their heads, and they apparently were as curious about my group as my students were about them.

This tract is preserved by the state of Florida, but only after environmental groups applied enough pressure to get the job done. In the Congaree it was also public pressure that worked, but not entirely to the satisfaction of those who would see it preserved.

The Congaree Swamp National Preserve Association and the Sierra Club had campaigned for a 70,000-acre tract of the Congaree to be set aside. Congress, acting under pressures from the timber industry and people little concerned with the environment, whittled the proposal down to 15,000 acres, less than one-fourth the initial area. At least 11,000 of those acres must look little different than they did at the time Columbus set sail for the New World. Here are bald cypress trees hundreds of years old with trunk circumferences up to twenty-five feet. Oak, sweetgum, loblolly pine, cottonwood, hickory, water tupelo—all form a patriarch forest, some state or national records, their canopies blotting out the sun except when weak wintery light filters through leafless branches. They call them the redwoods of the East.

A second rank of less stately trees—red maple, American holly, red mulberry— fill some of the spaces beneath the high canopy. And sometimes, in the lonely silent chambers of the cathedral woods, comes the staccato jackhammer of what may be the ivory-billed woodpecker, believed extinct for many years. Both the Congaree and Big Thicket have long been thought to be the final havens for these shy giant woodpeckers. The last one officially reported was spotted in the mid-1960s in the Big Thicket, but so numerous are reports from the Congaree of both sightings and chips from workings that many ornithologists believe this indeed could be a habitat for the great ivory-billed. Other rare creatures inhabit these forests: the panther, black bear, and, in the case of the Big Thicket, the Texas red wolf.

Unlike the Big Thicket, the forest floor of the Congaree is generally clear and easy to walk through, for instead of dead logs and brambles the understory consists of small trees and shrubs—pawpaw and spicebush mainly, but also blue beech, planer tree, blue-stem palmetto, and strawberry bush. Poison ivy vines as thick as an

43

arm ascend the great tree trunks and disappear in the canopies 150 feet above the forest floor. Other woody vines, some of them producing aerial roots which descend toward the ground in spidery veils, grow profusely. Thickets of switch cane are scattered, and there are even a few brakes of giant cane.

Along the stream banks of the Congaree River, which feeds the swamp, ghost-like sycamores dominate, while the flats along the cuts and dead-river lakes are rimmed by either bald cypress or tupelo gum and large overcup oak. The many low ridges that cut through the floodplain support thick stands of sweetgum, cherrybark oak, and holly. On the higher ridges and isolated rises of high ground along the swamp's edge, massive gigantic loblolly pines grow among the hardwoods, a rare occurrence in a hardwood swamp. Most of the loblolly appear to be fifty to seventy-five years old, indicating that some major disturbance—perhaps a fire—once cleared portions of the swamp, allowing the shade-intolerant pines to establish themselves. The pines are not reproducing themselves, however, and in time they will disappear. Their space in the forest will then be taken over by the pine ridge understory consisting of sweet bay, white ash and willow, laurel and water oak.

Surprisingly, the Congaree lacks large populations of wildlife. Wild turkeys, whitetail deer, river otters, raccoons, gray squirrels, and at least two poisonous snakes—the canebrake rattler and the cottonmouth moccasin—live here. Rare indeed are panther and black bear, both of which were numerous before the turn of the century. In recent years a group of scientists from the University of Tennessee spotted a large number of Mississippi kites along the river, but they have not been reported since.

So other than the possibility that the Congaree provides habitat for the ivory-billed woodpecker, its main attractions are the patriarch trees. They have stood hundreds of years. General Francis Marion, the legendary Swamp Fox of the American Revolution who staged guerilla raids from these wild places, paid tribute to them, saying: "I look at the venerable trees around me, and I know that I must not dishonor them." Many of the Swamp Fox's activities were centered around the Four Holes and Congaree swamps. Marion's men would hit suddenly and unexpectedly, then disappear into the swamp, where few armies dared to follow.

Opposite. *Ferns of the Okefenokee.*
Above. *The Okefenokee.*
Right. *Old growth in the Congaree Swamp,
South Carolina.*

An Okefenokee waterway.

Since the earliest American settlers touched land, man has staged an all-out battle against wilderness. It was something to be conquered. The first sawmill was built in 1608 at Jamestown. During the next two hundred years, most of the forests of the northeastern and Great Lakes states were stripped of big trees. Much was clear-cut to make way for agriculture. Around 1880, the timber industry moved south. During the next thirty years, the southern swamp forests suffered great losses, with the biggest and best trees going first; the others soon followed. In 1909 the southern forests produced more than 21 billion board feet of lumber, nearly half of the nation's total production. By 1917 there were more than 100 million acres of cutover land in the South. By this time, the lumber companies had been joined by the pulp and paper industry. Most of the virgin timber was gone.

There were signs of decline, but when World War II came along, demand increased, and again the profiteering timber barons stripped the forests. By 1945, most of the South's old-growth timber was gone from the piney woods of the uplands as well as from the river-bottom swamps. The Congaree Swamp and the Four Holes would have been among them except for one man who once took a trip to Yellowstone National Park and was so impressed he became a dyed-in-the-wool conservationist. His name was Francis Beidler.

Beidler was the son of a Pennsylvania Mennonite farmer who had moved to Chicago, became a carpenter, and gravitated into the lumber business. Young Beidler followed in his father's footsteps, and in 1875 he took a month off to explore the West. The experience produced a lifelong commitment to conservation. In 1907, he went to Europe to study European timber conservation techniques and, upon returning, applied some of what he had learned to his own timber holdings. And when the timber began to run out in the Midwest, Beidler explored the South.

Even before he went to Europe, he came to South Carolina by train to explore the swamp forests of the Santee, Wateree, and Congaree rivers. He entered despite warnings from local residents he would never come out of the swamp alive. Legends and superstitions ran rampant in the area, and the natives were as fearful of the swamp as they would have been of Hades itself. But Beidler did survive, and returned to Chicago so impressed with what he saw that he borrowed a million dollars from the University of Chicago with which to purchase South Carolina swamp forests. The Santee, Congaree, and Four Holes swamps were included in this transaction.

During a fifteen-year period from 1890 to 1905, Beidler purchased more than 100,000 acres of swamp forest in South Carolina and formed the Santee River Cypress Lumber Company. The lumber company built a sawmill and began cutting cypress. The huge trees were girdled so the sap would run out and lighten them enough to float. Then they were cut during a dry season and the logs floated out of the swamps to the sawmill during the next high water. But there were many problems. Some years there were no floods, and the trees lay where they had fallen. Mosquitos were horrendous during the hot-weather months. Malaria broke out, and the milling crews refused or were unable to work. In 1914, after only a short period of operation, the sawmill was closed. The last cypress logs in the Congaree were cut in 1910.

All timber operations in the Congaree ceased, and the forest grew silent and more stately. The patriarch trees became even more awesome. Then, in 1969, the timber harvesting resumed. Long before then, Francis Beidler had died; the timberlands passed to his heirs and mainly to his son, Francis Beidler II. Along with the timberlands, the junior Beidler inherited something else from his father: a healthy respect for conservation.

"Conservation," he said, "used to be considered a folly similar to the holding of a hot potato which should be dropped. In opposition to this view, my father convinced my mother and me the forests were a vital national asset that should be preserved, and we formed a tiny minority in the midst of universal disapproval."

But the taxes and expenses continued. So the Beidlers offset some of that expense by leasing the forest to the Cedar Creek Hunt Club, whose members helped maintain the roads and police the property against trespassers.

During the early 1940s, a great hydroelectric plant was needed for the war effort in this area, and it was decided to build it on the Santee River. To provide that power, the Santee would have to be dammed. The Santee Swamp, toward the sea from the Congaree, would be inundated. The land was condemned; the Beidlers were forced to sell at prices they felt were far below fair value. And besides, the flooding of the Santee Swamp violated every premise the elder Beidler had instilled in his family. Francis Beidler II was bitter.

But he did negotiate with the National Audubon Society and the Nature Conservancy, which sought to purchase and preserve for all time the Four Holes Swamp, some thirty-five miles northwest of Charleston. As the last major undisturbed cypress-tupelo black-water swamp in the world, its preservation was an important factor.

The Four Holes was distinctly different from the Congaree or the Santee. Formed by the wave action and tidal currents of the pre-Pleistocene sea, which carved scarplike bluffs of its trench and built the offshore bar that deflected the old Four Holes River out of its seaward course, the Four Holes is the home of great buttressed giants. Cypress knees more than eight feet tall form an understory forest suggestive of the nubby limbs of saguaro cactus forests. Four Holes and its great god forest are nurtured by a network of interconnected small channels and lagoons and myriad springs.

In the spring of 1974, 3500 acres of Four Holes Swamp, including roughly 1800 acres of virgin bald cypress and tupelo gum unmatched anywhere else, were dedicated as the Francis Beidler Memorial Forest. It was a fitting monument; today it is an Audubon sanctuary, and has been expanded to 5819 acres.

It was most appropriate that the Four Holes be preserved, for it is one of the greatest undisturbed swamps of its kind. Scientists come from many parts of the nation to study the Four Holes. Charles H. Wharton, a former professor of biology at Georgia State University and author of *The Southern River Swamp,* describes the Four Holes as a "jewel ecosystem."

The campaign to save the Four Holes was no easy one. While the Beidler family was anxious to have it preserved, they would not simply donate the land. The price tag was $1.45 million. A number of money-making schemes were established. The Columbia chapter of the Audubon Society conducted a sale of pileated woodpecker prints by artist Anne Richardson of Charleston and donated the profits toward the purchase. Nonetheless, the transaction practically drained the Audubon coffers and left few funds for other matters. More recently, however, some facilities—including canoe trails and a boardwalk through a small portion of the swamp—have been opened to the public, as well as a fine visitor's center.

Although the swamp gives the immediate impression that there is no understory, more than 120 species of woody plants were counted in the area by John Dennis working with The Nature Conservancy. Among them is the green-fly orchid, its petaled blooms picturesquely spread on the limbs of hardwoods throughout the swamp. Resurrection ferns and cardinal flowers grow along the main streams and add a rare beauty dating back to Pleistocene times. Great clumps of poison ivy fold outward from stumps like giant bouquets. And from the canopied chambers of this inner sanctum come the calls of Carolina wrens, blue-gray gnatcatchers, and prothonotary warblers, punctuated by the great god call of the pileated woodpecker. Some say the rare Bachman's warbler lives here, too.

Twilight in the Okefenokee.

The Four Holes is filled with non-toxic but vicious brown watersnakes and lazy, venomous cottonmouth moccasins. River otters are common; they feast upon a multitude of fish—stumpknockers, largemouth bass, red breasts or bream, crayfish, gar, and the *Chologaster,* an ancestor of the blind cave fish similar to those found in underground streams. Raccoons and alligators are also residents of this swamp.

Although the Four Holes must bow to the Congaree for most of the huge record trees, it is filled with towering cypress and tupelo monuments, some taller than a ten-story building, with a canopy so dense that sunlight seldom penetrates except during winter. It was the same when General Francis Marion sought seclusion here; the same when the Natchez Indians lived within its chambers.

The Four Holes has played an extensive historical role in the area. It may have been the last sanctuary of the Natchez. Entries in the Journal of Commons of the state of Mississippi show the Colonial House of Commons decided on September 16, 1733, that the Natchez Indians "now encamped at Four Holes Swamp be sent as soon as possible to scout about Port Royal." Later, the Natchez were placed on an island reservation in Port Royal Sound. Pieces of Indian pottery, arrowheads, and other artifacts are occasionally found in the swamp or in fields close by.

About the same time efforts were gaining momentum to save the Four Holes, more than a thousand miles away efforts were underway to save the last remaining segments of the Texas Big Thicket. And in south Florida a similar effort was being made to set aside a good portion of the Big Cypress Swamp, which already had lost virtually all its virgin timber. The only noteworthy undisturbed forest was in the Fakahatchee Strand of the Big Cypress. And in the Big Thicket, about all that remained were scattered remnants, the best along the banks of the Neches River and Pine Island Bayou.

When the Alabama-Coushatta Indians, whose reservation is now a part of the Big Thicket, first came to this area around 1800, the Thicket embraced some three million acres—all of it virgin forest, grassland, marsh, and swampland. It was easy to find even one hundred years later, for it was a formidable, dense curtain of jungle that seemingly stretched forever. But that soon changed; the Thicket was used and abused, sawed, chopped, mowed, drilled into, and burned over. But despite man's long, ruthless campaign to convert this wild place to commerce, remnants of the Big Thicket do indeed still exist.

In the autumn of 1974, Congress gave the Big Thicket a new lease on life by creating the Big Thicket National Preserve, administered by the National Park Service. By so doing, it bought some time for conservationists and environmental organizations that, for years, had campaigned for its preservation. As one member of the Big Thicket Association has pointed out, "The battle has not yet been won, but victory looms upon the horizon."

While some 84,550 acres in twelve separate units were purchased by the National Park Service, only a small portion of that contains any virgin timber . . . in fact, the only portions left undisturbed by man are those parts too inaccessible for him to easily cut over. In those remote areas, vegetation consists of palmetto, live oak, virgin beech, magnolia, sassafras, dogwood, wild grapevines, and giant loblolly pines. Among the original growth of the Thicket is a great magnolia tree believed to be more than one thousand years old, a holly tree eighty feet tall recognized as the largest of its kind in the world, and more than one thousand species of fungi and algae as well as some forty varieties of wild orchids. Ferns grow profusely, and there's an extensive variety of herbs ranging from ginseng to wax myrtle. Scarlet buckeye, wild phlox, wild azalea, wild iris, and trumpet vine grow profusely.

The wild woodland of the Big Thicket quickly is regaining its original stature now that it's being preserved, for the soil is rich and the climate favorable for fast and

51

lush growth. In fact, the Big Thicket itself has a moderating influence on the climate of the region. It provides a buffer to cold northers, local tornadoes, and destructive hurricanes blowing up from the Gulf of Mexico. Winters are generally mild, and summers are cooler and more pleasant than those of the drier and more open adjacent woodlands deeper inland.

From the beginning of this century, conservationists were concerned about the preservation of the Big Thicket, but the movement groundswelled in the late 1960s and early 1970s. Part of their concern was over the area of tree giants, many of them national or state champions, an area similar in this respect to the Congaree. Here grow the world's largest red bay, sweet-leaf, black hickory, American holly, planer tree, sparkleberry, eastern red cedar, and two-wing silverbell. Spearheading the move for preservation was the Big Thicket Association, headquartered at Saratoga, Texas, in the midst of the Thicket.

Because of its wildness, the Big Thicket for many years was a refuge for Indians, outlaws, runaway slaves, and army deserters. According to one story, Sam Houston, during the Texas Revolution, planned to disappear with his army into this wild sanctuary if he lost the Battle of San Jacinto. Those who took refuge here lived off the land, on wild game and wild honey; there's even a town named Honey Island where fugitives brought honey to be traded on the black market for goods and wares they needed in the swamp.

The Big Thicket has long been home to the ivory-billed woodpecker and the Texas red wolf (both are still believed to be living in the remote wild sections there). It also harbors such rarities of the wildlife kingdom as Swainson's warbler, the red-cockaded woodpecker, the pileated woodpecker, and virtually the only black bear in all of eastern Texas. There are panthers, and bobcats, and, as late as the 1930s, jaguars and the Mexican ocelots roamed there. Possibly some still do.

Not all swamp forests are found in the South or southeastern United States, however. Some are considerably removed, such as Goll Woods in northwestern Ohio, a remnant of the Great Black Swamp. Containing only eighty acres, it represents a virgin forest of bur oak, white oak, cottonwood, and a few other species—white and black ash, tulip trees, maple and butternut.

Goll Woods would long ago have disappeared had it not been for one man—Peter Goll. In August 1834 Goll came to settle here from his native Germany, purchasing the land for $1.25 an acre. He cleared a portion of it to farm, but left untouched many acres in what he always called "the big woods." For four generations, Goll Woods remained in the Goll family. All of them loved the big trees, and they carefully guarded the Big Woods from a multitude of timber operators.

In 1966, The Nature Conservancy and the Ohio Department of Natural Resources purchased the woods and three years later dedicated it Goll Woods. It was, they claimed, the only remaining section of the original Black Swamp that covered thousands upon thousands of acres since glacial times.

In neighboring Pennsylvania is another virgin swamp forest—a mountain swamp—with great hemlocks. Called the East Branch Swamp and containing only 186 acres, it's located in Clinton County.

None of these are as unique, however, as the Alakai Swamp forest of the Eden isle of Kauai, Hawaii. The natives call it "the swamp in the clouds," for it is located in the crater of a volcano in the shadow of Mount Waialeale. For centuries it has been

Above. *Blossoms of the carnivorous pitcher plant.*
Right. *A golden club in the Okefenokee.*

Left. *Female anhinga preening in the Big Cypress.*
Below. *Wild azalea in the Okefenokee.*

largely inaccessible, which accounts partially for the fact that it has been left undisturbed. The general topography and the densely entangled, junglelike growth was enough to discourage all but the most determined hikers. On three sides steep cliffs, called *palis* in Hawaiian, bound the swamp, but there are a few approaches with less steep ridges.

Another reason it remains largely unexplored by man are the rains. "It scares people to think of experiencing a thirty-inch rainfall in twenty-four hours," said an official of the U.S. Forest Service Pacific Institute in Honolulu. "And that's what happens in the swamp. It can rain so hard up there you think you're swimming underwater if you're caught in it." It gets from 200 to 225 inches of rain each year, or about 18 to 20 feet.

The Alakai, approximately nine miles long and three miles wide, is about four thousand feet above sea level. Until recent times, little was known about it, but scientists have now accomplished some studies and made enough field trips into the area to know just how unique it really is. Giant ferns grow twenty feet tall; moss clings a foot thick on the trunks of the trees. The principal tree is the *ohia lehua,* which grows no more than fifty feet tall there because of the saturated condition of the clay and peat soil. It normally grows to about eighty feet.

Even this remote swamp forest is changing. Foresters are most concerned about a changing ecosystem where heavy infiltrations of blackberry vines, firebush, and lantana weeds are moving into certain areas. Wherever a clearing develops, either by fire, uprooted trees, or the ruthless rootings of wild hogs, weeds and vines capture the area with growth so dense nothing else can survive. Robert Nelson, director of the Institute of Pacific Islands Forestry of the U.S. Forest Service, believes this could have critical results in the Alakai and perhaps a devastating effect upon some of its endangered wildlife. The State Division of Forestry has begun a program of control against such intrusions, and hopefully it will be sufficient to stabilize the forest.

The endangered wildlife mainly consists of a half dozen or so species of nearly extinct birds. Among them are the *Drepanididae* (honeycreepers), the small Kauai thrush (found only in the Alakai, where it lives a largely secretive life), the *Elepaio* or Hawaiian flycatcher, the *Kauaioo,* the sicklebill or Hawaiian woodpecker, and the oui thickbill. Several of these species were once found throughout the Hawaiian Islands, but now are only found in the Alakai Swamp and then only rarely.

The swamp forest is an unusual place, whether it be in the strands of the Big Cypress, the mountain swamps of Appalachia, the riverbottom Congaree, or the Alakai. Their growth is lush, their wildlife often unique, and they present an ecotone dramatically different than most wild woodlands offer—a world in which anyone would feel a trespasser.

Soleduck Falls on the Soleduck River in the Olympic Forest, one of the most beautiful waterfalls in America.

THREE

The Rainforest

Nothing else on earth faintly resembles a temperate rainforest. Along river valleys carrying glacial meltwater to the Pacific Ocean from Washington's high Olympic mountain range are three distinct rainforests. They are magnificent entities of green, so rich that they virtually consume the spirit.

Before the timber barons and clearcutters, most of Washington's Olympic Peninsula was an idyllic forest environment, a wooded paradise. The three primary rainforest regions cloaking the three river valleys—the Hoh, Quinault, and Queets— were the jewels of one of nature's finest showpiece. They still are, but they are only yards away in many instances from the clearly defined work of the tree butchers. Clearcuts occur in all parts of the peninsula, except within the boundaries of the Olympic National Park itself—though in several well-documented instances since it was established by President Theodore Roosevelt, strong campaigns have been mounted to allow cutting within the park.

Today, the park has been designated—and rightfully so—an International Biosphere Park. It is without question one of the most impressive parks not only in America, but the world.

My very first visit to the Olympic Peninsula was in 1966; my family and I were returning from a summer's work in Alaska. It was mid-August and the children would soon be expected in school back in the Midwest. But there was still time for a few days' visit there. We stayed in the Lake Crescent Lodge, set in the midst of the park, surrounded by mountains. Created by glaciers during the Ice Age, the lake was deep, clear, and inviting. My oldest son, David, and oldest daughter, Dianne, who were both under twelve at that time, were anxious to take a dip after a summer of Alaska's frigid waters. So they could hardly wait to dive into these enticing waters

The Hall of Mosses on the Hoh Rainforest of the Olympic Peninsula.

"down south." Never did it occur to them these might be icy waters as well. But they discovered that the lake was quite frigid, and soon were sitting on the shore nursing their goosebumps.

Since it was a sunny day (which doesn't occur frequently on the Olympic Peninsula), the emerald-green lake was rimmed with the reflective forest of big trees. US Highway 101, which circled the peninsula, ran behind the lodge, and from our vantage point we could count the armadas of logging trucks carrying timber off to the mills. At that time, most of it was heading for the domestic market; in later years, substantial amounts of it would be heading for Japan, and still later, to Japanese factory ships just beyond the three-mile-limit. There it would be processed into all kinds of wood products and resold to markets in the United States. The big trees, the ancient ones, were fast disappearing. The whine of the chain saw and the echo of the ax were taking an irrevocable toll. Trees that had come to be monuments, each far more impressive than any monument erected by man, were crashing to the ground in substantial numbers. To turn back seemed impossible.

Moss growing on the heavy bark of old-growth Ponderosa pine.

I left the Olympic Peninsula of the sixties in considerable dismay at what I saw there, and I did not return again for a dozen years. If I had not fallen in love with it the first time, I most certainly did in 1978. I had been working my way around the United States coast, all the way from Maine, working on a book of mine entitled *The Island*. I had gamely pushed my way along for more than a year when I reached the state of Washington and the Olympic Peninsula in May. Washington doesn't have many offshore islands, and when I had completed my work on them, I turned to look at the rainforest on the mainland, realizing the special place it had earned in my heart after all these years.

Day after day, I drove inland, up the Hoh and the Quinault to the end of the roads. Then I hiked the trails into quiet green chambers that dripped tears and saturated the carpeted floor most of the time.

It was true rainforest. Twelve years ago I had not come to know this place as I now got to know it. The moss-covered logs, the big-leaf maple trees with club moss so thick you could ram your fist into it without touching the trunk of the tree, the thicket of tall ferns surrounded with shamrock and more rampant growth than you could ever imagine . . . the whole forest was a dripping sponge. It rained and rained and rained.

In my small Chinook motorhome, I would lie in bed mornings and listen to the constant drip on the fiberglass roof. One morning I was awakened at dawn by the strangest sound. It was a chewing sound, and when I pulled back the curtains to peer outside, there were a dozen or so of the finest big Roosevelt elk grazing around me I could imagine. The grass was lush, and their grazing created a unique sound effect; it was marvelous. What an awakening!

Much of the rain in this area is not the kind of rain most people who live in other places are used to. There are no downpours here—at least, I've never experienced one. It's a misty rain. I spent the whole month of May that year on the Olympic Peninsula, with maybe one sojourn into Seattle to play tourist. During that month, the sun was shining a high percentage of the time. But it also rained good amounts. I came to call it "dry rain," for one could, most days, work outdoors for long periods of time without raingear and still not get wet. Not soaked, anyway.

I continued to work, taking pictures in the rain of some of this magnificent forest. My cameras were damp most of the time. And I never lost any film because of the rain. The temperatures were generally warm—into the sixties most days—so the comfort index was a very positive one. When I wanted to dry out, I merely moved my campsite over to the northern side of the peninsula in the rain shadow of the Olympics.

In the rainforest on the west end of the peninsula, the rainfall is just under 200 inches a year. Remarkably, at Sequim, in the rain shadow, it's officially desert, with a rainfall of approximately fourteen to seventeen inches a year. So I would set up camp at the KOA between Port Angeles and Sequim and dry everything out for a day or two while I worked in the upper levels of the park at Deer Park and Hurricane Ridge. There was still a good eight feet of snow in the parking lot of the Visitor's Center at Hurricane Ridge, which offers a mountaincrest view of the Olympics. Down at Port Angeles, the roadsides and meadows were filled with temperate wildflower gardens. Driving time between the two points was just about twenty minutes. So I could actually drive from a balmy springtime day to heavy winter snow in no time at all. I loved it.

If I wanted sun, I could generally find it at Sequim or Port Angeles, but if I wanted rain, I could have that as well by just driving a couple of hours west to the town of Forks on the edge of the rainforest.

To truly know the rainforest, however, one does not run to the drier climates to warm up and dry out. One stays, like the plants and trees and animals that live here. And one then learns what it's like to live in a true rainforest environment. The three stream valleys where they exist are nearly parallel. The shallow rivers meander in a snakelike path along the floors of these U-shaped corridors, which are nearly a mile wide.

Sometimes a river changes course, particularly during spring floods when the banks become swollen and the waters more swift and powerful. It leaves behind a soggy path of land that was previously riverbed. This then becomes the incubator of forest yet to come. In another thousand years or so, the bare surface will have become a thick forest of towering trees, springy mosses, meadows of shamrock and fern, and

Opposite. *At higher elevations in the Olympic Mountain Range, old growth blends with younger trees to form an interesting pattern.*

a revel of tangled plants—oxalis, vanilla leaf, foamflower, bedstraw, and liverworts. The process of birth is indeed slow, but it is continuous and sometimes overlapping.

Generally, foresters say it can be divided into four distinctive stages. During the first stage, grasses and willows grow in the thin, gravelly soil and are soon followed by alders. In the second stage, bigger deciduous trees such as cottonwoods and maples, as well as the evergreen spruces, shade out the alders. Young hemlocks, too, begin to appear. As the trees start to crowd one another, the forest gradually thins its ranks to spruce and hemlock and, finally, to the more shade tolerant of the two, hemlock. The forest has now reached its permanent, or climax, stage. Barring external interference, no other trees will now crowd out the hemlocks. This is the final stage; the development of the woodland has reached its apex.

The beginnings of a forest yet to come is most fascinating, but it's often unimpressive to those looking for outstanding beauty or drama. The luxuriant forest begins with velvet grass, sheep's sorrel, sedge, wild strawberries, and western millet. Willow trees may soon follow, growing rapidly and stabilizing the land with a maze of roots lacing together the pebbles. After all, the river may rise again and seek to tear away the very foundations of silted deposits which will become the basis for the new forest.

One night when I was camping on the Hoh that spring, the river was only slightly higher than normal from glacial melt in the high country, but it was far from flooding. I was awakened at 2 A.M. by the sudden and unexpected clattering and clashing of boulders and rocks in the nearby stream. It seemed to be occurring only in one location. I got up and peered out of my tent. A faint moon hung in partially foggy skies, but nothing else seemed to be unusual. The river water looked no different than the day before. But the rocks kept moving, cracking and clashing against one another for more than an hour. It was as though the riverbed had suddenly, for some unexplained reason, come alive. It stopped just as unexpectedly as it had begun, and there was not another sound from them the remainder of the night, or on subsequent nights I camped there.

That taught me that the river is very much alive, and constantly changing. Consequently, the plant life that emerges early faces a struggle every moment of every day. Once the plants have begun to grow, they trap silt brought by the waters. The grasses form mats and the silt becomes more land, capable of developing much-

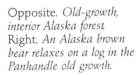

Opposite. *Old-growth, interior Alaska forest.* Right. *An Alaska brown bear relaxes on a log in the Panhandle old growth.*

needed humus. Spring floods bring more sand. In a few years, the first real trees—the red alders whose thin roots allow them to exist in shallow soil—begin to grow. By means of bacteria in their root systems, the alders extract nitrogen from the air, then add decomposing leaves and wood to prepare a bed for other plants and trees to use.

A period of some twenty years may pass before the alders begin to dominate the land, then another half century may pass before other big-trees-to-be like the Douglas fir or Sitka spruce seedlings will begin to challenge the alder's position. Two hundred more years may come and go before these giants shade out the understory; thus, the beginning of the climax forest. In the interim, large leaf maples may have grown for a generation or two, developing the thick spongy club mosses that cling to them.

From the very beginning of the rainforest, as with most forests, competition is fierce. But few forests offer such diversity of competition. Surrounding me at times when I have visited there are more than 1200 plant species, competing on every square inch of soil for light, moisture, and nutrients. Because there is so much moisture, and because the soil is deep and rich, growth comes easy. Here, for instance, ferns act as epiphytes, marching straight up the sides of living trees, finding a life platform in even the tiniest crevices in the bark of the forest monarchs. They are not parasitic; they will pass their entire lives attached to their hosts but extracting nothing from them. No niche that offers support and space is left unoccupied. This is the reason the rainforest is so unusually interesting to me.

The foundation of the forest, at any stage after its initial beginning when trees are yet to grow, is humus. This absorbent stratum holds rain and melting snow until it soaks down through the ground and into animal burrows, wormholes, ant channels, and passages left by decaying roots. The forest becomes a vast reservoir of water that seeps down through the earth, resurfacing at clear, cool springs. Thus, the forest stabilizes stream flow and protects the watershed, something the tree cutters fail to recognize.

One cannot, of course, stand still and watch the forest grow around him. In my own situation, however, it was much easier, for I would intermittently leave the forest and return, sometimes years later, to witness the changes that had taken place. I could also experience the stages of forest growth in a single day by merely walking away from the riverbank. Since the time these valleys were formed by glaciers and then eroded in time by the rivers, parts of the valleys have already been through the forest succession or are in one or another of its stages at the present time. To walk away from the river toward the upward limits of the side of the valley is to move backward through generations of forest—moving hundreds of years in just hundreds of feet. On the other hand, if you study the new land formed by the river, you can see into the future and visualize new forest to come a thousand, two thousand years into the future.

You get a feel for the true nature of time in these woods. You reach an understanding that if you live to be eighty, it is merely a blink of the eye to a forest where trees 1500 years old or more still sway in the breezes off the Pacific. You need to visit the forest of great trees every few years just to properly readjust your perspective on time.

A rainforest is in some ways a state of mind. It is more than the mere presence of certain species of plants and animals. Their interaction with each other and with the total environment is much more significant. The grotesque and weirdly beautiful

Above. *Dogwood on the Olympic Peninsula.*
Above right. *This ptarmigan is changing from summer to winter dress during an Alaskan autumn.*
Right. *Bull moose, Alaska.*

A coastal rainforest near Juneau, Alaska.

A lone bald eagle almost lost in the expanse of coastal Alaska old-growth woods.

A red fox, intent upon the noise of a ground squirrel, is one of the inhabitants of the old-growth woods of Alaska.

big-leaf maples, clothed and draped in verdant green moss and ferns, set the stage for the purest stands of rainforest, but there are other elements, too. Consider the Sitka spruce, for instance, and other giants that form the nucleus of these woods.

As a species, the Sitka spruce ranges from Kodiak, Alaska, to Mendocino County, California, north of San Francisco. But only on the Olympic Peninsula does it consistently reach such awesome size. For years, the world record was thought to be a tree in the Hoh Valley that measured more than thirteen feet in diameter, so huge that eight men with outstretched arms, fingertip to fingertip, could not reach around it. Some time later, a greater Sitka spruce, measuring fifteen feet in diameter, was found near the little town of Seaside, Oregon. Subsequently, two more were found in the Queets Valley which towered over the Oregon tree. Who knows what other giants are yet to be found in the coastal forest? A spokesman for the British Columbia Ministry of Forests says it has thousands of giant Sitka spruce, but it doesn't know how large they are. The ministry has documented their existence from satellite readings from space, but thus far has been unable to ascertain their diameter. "We know," the spokesman said, "we have trees that were seedlings at Year One A.D."

In the summer of 1991, while conducting a nature photography workshop with a dozen or so students among the big trees, we documented on film a western cedar exceeding sixty-eight feet in circumference. It looked more like a fluted giant pipe organ than a tree with draped aprons of xylem adorning its structure. Even standing twenty feet away, it seemed unbelievable that anything this huge could exist on the planet. Most of us stood in awed silence; if we spoke at all, it was in hushed whispers, as though we might disturb, in some way, the tranquility in which this giant lived.

All over the Olympic Peninsula, where greedy timbermen have not been, the mammoth trees live. More gigantic trees of more different species grow here than at any other place in all the world. Tropical rainforests in Australia, New Zealand, Africa, and South America are generally more varied than those found here, but their trees are not as large.

The Sitka spruce is not the only one holding records in the coastal forest; the largest known western hemlock in the world stands in the Quinault Valley, and the largest Douglas fir in the Queets. In the Hoh Valley is the largest red alder, and the largest red cedar stands in the fringe of the rainforest near Kalaloch, close by the Pacific. One almost as large is located on a hillside above Lake Quinault.

While the truest temperate rainforest lies in the three river valleys on the Olympic Peninsula—and it is also the most impressive—other rainforest environments extend far beyond that. On Alaska's Kodiak Island, one summer I camped on a fringe of rainforest that in many ways resembled the forest I had known on the Olympic Peninsula. The trees were certainly not as large, because of the scant soil, but the club moss and fern adornments and even the same species of trees surely reminded me of rainforest. In parts of the Alaskan Panhandle, the old-growth rainforest begins again, extending down through coastal British Columbia in Canada.

The rainforest is not rich in wildlife habitat. One sees blacktail deer in some abundance and there are numerous little chickarees or Douglas squirrels that tear around the trees, squeaking their excitement; lots of ravens, too, and the occasional pileated woodpecker and goshawk. One of the most important residents as far as the longevity of the old-growth forest is concerned is the northern spotted owl. It has become a controversial subject of the entire Pacific Northwest and coastal Canada as well since it was placed on the endangered species list of the U.S. Fish and Wildlife Service.

The northern spotted owl, which I have never seen in all my years of working in the Pacific Northwest and which many of my friends who are natives there have never seen either, can only survive, it seems, in old growth. It makes its nest in natural cavities that result when storms break off the tops of trees in old-growth forests. Without these snags, spotted owls cannot survive. The snags, in other words, are as necessary for the propagation of the spotted owl as the nurse log is to the propagation of the rainforest community. Both are important.

Consequently, thousands of acres of woods within the boundaries of the U.S. Forest Service have been taken out of production; no cutting will be done there among old-growth stands until the spotted owl controversy is settled. So this little owl may be the catalyst for saving much of the old-growth timber of the Pacific Northwest. Only about 10 percent of it, outside the national park, is left unharmed anyway. The timber industry is not at rest, however, and wants to cut even that remaining percentage.

Throughout the forest are nurse logs, which are a fascinating delight. Delicate mosses and lichens carpet the entire forest and where there are old nurse logs—that is, ones which have been on the forest floor for twenty years or more—the green carpet covers them in undulating waves. From them grow ferns, mushrooms, and shrub seedlings that reach up to form a second level. Young trees like maples, spruces, hemlocks, all firmly rooted in the decaying wood, make up the canopy. In places, I have encountered nurse logs from which as many as forty trees grow, some of them reaching heights of forty to fifty feet. Eventually, the nurse logs completely decay and

69

Above. *The Olympic Mountains.*
Below. *The Elwha River in the Olympic National Park.*

Lake Crescent, in the midst of the land of big trees on the Olympic Peninsula, is a glacier-created lake with depths ranging upwards of 500 feet.

become a part of the humus of the forest floor, of course, and no physical evidence is left of them. Hundreds of years in the future, these trees which grew from a nurse log will fall and become nurse logs themselves. Thus the cycle continues.

Jerry Franklin of the University of Washington's School of Forestry has published studies on the importance of nurse logs in the forest community. "They are a primal force," says Franklin, "and must be considered as necessary in a true forest environment."

The temperate rainforest, naturally, differs from the tropical rainforest. The deciduous trees in the Olympic rainforest are predominantly black cottonwood, red alder, and big-leaf maple. The tropical rainforest trees are entirely different, with channel surface drainage and tips that end in dripping points in the leaves. The brush of the Olympic forest is mostly vine maple, huckleberry, and sapling conifers; in the tropical forest it is tree ferns and bamboo. Superabundant moisture characterizes both forests, however; in the tropics rain falls evenly throughout the year and temperatures hold so steady there's an absence of growth rings in many species. In the Olympics, the rainfall during summer is light, but heavy in winter with marine fog, much of the time, providing much moisture.

Nurse log.

Logs carried down the streams from either cuttings or "wind-downs" piled high during winter storms on Pacific beaches.

The tropical rainforests often are characterized as jungle because of the dense growth and steamy atmosphere. The Olympic rainforest does have dense growth, but at the same time there is a decided openness about it as well. You can easily walk in most places of the Olympic rainforest; not so in the rainforests of New Zealand, the Amazon, or many other locations.

While there are strong adversaries debating the future of the Olympic rainforest outside the national park, the beauty and value of this area was recognized long ago by many people of leadership and influence. Teddy Roosevelt, although often torn between hunting and conservation, was impressed by the fact that an elk had recently been named after him by famed naturalist C. Hart Merriam. Two days before leaving the presidency Roosevelt signed a proclamation setting aside 600,000 acres as sanctuary for those animals. Under this proclamation, that area was designated a national monument, but one which still allowed hunting and logging. Thankfully, logging pressures were not as great since there was less public demand in those days.

It was some twenty-nine years later that President Franklin D. Roosevelt visited the monument, stayed at Lake Crescent Lodge, and heard arguments from foresters and conservationists on the future of the monument. When he returned to Washington, he immediately petitioned Congress to establish the kind of protected national park that would be the biggest anyone had dared propose for the peninsula.

This clearcut near the town of Forks on the Olympic Peninsula dates back several years.

A logging truck carries old growth to a mill.

Even before FDR's visit, the Olympic monarchs had been in grave danger. During World War I, President Woodrow Wilson halved the size of the monument set aside by Teddy Roosevelt to just 300,000 acres on the grounds that its Sitka spruce was needed for building airplanes. The Army formed a unit called the Spruce Division manned by volunteer soldiers with experience as lumberjacks and sawmill operators. During the summer of 1918, more than ten thousand of these men were hard at work on the Olympic Peninsula cutting down Sitka spruce.

Fortunately, the war ended before the Spruce Division reached the finest sections of rainforest. It was a narrow escape for the big trees. Timber interests then concentrated on holdings near the coast; the upriver forests were spared until Olympic National Park was created by FDR and the Congress in 1938. Even then the logging companies, once more interested in the mountain flanks, pressed for legislation that would allow them inside the park. The great trees, just out of reach on broad valley floors, still entice the loggers.

Periodically invoking some crisis or another (either in the national interest or the energy crisis or sometimes even the state of the local economy) the timber barons continue their endless lobbying. During the early stages of the spotted owl controversy, a group of loggers at Forks erected a monument near the center of town resembling a burial site with a cross bearing statues of a few spotted owls. A sign

73

read: "Here lies the future of our children." The monument has since been removed. The view this reflects is understandable, since Forks to this point has been almost totally dependent upon the timber industry, but those with an eye toward the future must know that sooner or later the cutting of big trees must stop.

An assistant in my Olympic rainforest nature photography workshop, Bill Rinehart of Port Angeles, has lived there all his life. He is an accountant, and so firmly aware of the role timber plays in the economy of virtually the entire Olympic Peninsula. Yet, as a lover of nature and photography, he is torn. If the cutting of big trees is stopped, the total economic picture at both Port Angeles and Forks will change dramatically. It will be necessary to find another way to bolster it. Already residents there are improving their tourism program; at the moment it seems the quickest and least damaging manner to do it.

I live in my own primitive forest in Florida, consisting mainly of huge live oaks dating back 400 years. But over the past ten years, when snows are still melting in the high country of the Olympics and the high meadows are decorated with wild-flowers, I come to the Pacific Northwest to pay homage to these great trees. From the time my plane lands at Seattle, I can hardly wait to rent a vehicle and escape to one of my favorite spots. It's one which few people know, under the canopy of old friends that stand 300 feet tall and twelve feet in diameter.

I pitch my tent on the soft, padded forest floor and often lie there with my head sticking outside the entrance, gazing at the sky and trees. While I realize black bear and mountain lion are my unseen neighbors here, it is the majesty of these monarchs that instills in me an identification with immortality I cannot explain.

Never before has greater attention been paid to the place Sierra Club founder John Muir called "the noblest forests of the world." Hopefully, the big trees, every one of the monarchs standing at this time, will be allowed to tower over the Olympic Peninsula until they are annihilated by natural causes.

Opposite. *A central Alaska primeval forest sunset.*

FOUR

The North Woods

In the midst of the North Woods, which extend from Hudson Bay southward into the Great Lakes territory, there is a relatively small tract of old-growth white and red pine. This old growth is the nucleus of what was North America's most extensive ancient forest just 200 years ago. It's affectionately called The Lost Forty, a reference to an honest 1886 mistake in survey engineering. Without such an error, it, too, might have been lost to Paul Bunyan's ax and saw.

Today, The Lost Forty contains trees 300 to 400 years old that tower 100 feet above the thin soil covering the Canadian Shield in northern Minnesota's Chippewa National Forest. The forest, named after a tribe of Indians who have lived for centuries in the northern Minnesota and North Dakota area, is only part of some 7000 acres of old growth in the Chippewa. It is all being preserved for posterity.

It was with some understanding and pride that I wandered up from Bemidji to Blackduck one spring. The road to Blackduck was modern America, but a few miles out of town the way became a mere tunnel through the woods. I came to a town called Alvwood. Shortly, the first true old growth presented itself—sentry trees towering to the sky and shading out the sun. Seed cones were scattered upon the ground, and there was the unmistakable fresh scent of pine in the air. It was wonderful, and if I ever had any doubts or anxiety about getting here, they quickly disappeared.

At a small parking lot I left my car. From this point, I would experience the great forest on foot. I followed the trail as it disappeared into the woods, and suddenly I was amid towering stands of red and white pines. The understory was almost nonexistent. This, I decided, was cathedral country.

Not all of the North Woods is cathedral country, or ever was. Even when the French Voyageurs traveled well-worn trails through the woods and lakes country, of

Opposite. *Boundary Waters, located on the Minnesota-Canadian border, has extensive old growth and thousands of lakes.*

western Ontario and Minnesota, much of the forest was stunted. Seldom, if ever, do we find trees, even the 400-year-old ones, rising to more than 100 feet. Foresters of the Pacific Northwest or of the awesome redwoods and sequoias of California would not be impressed. But for middle North America, these are behemoths.

The chief reason trees in the North Woods do not grow larger, I'm told, is the thin soil. Only about ten inches of soil covers the sheer rock of the Canadian Shield all the way from the tundra areas west and north of Hudson Bay to parts of Minnesota, Michigan, and Wisconsin. The larger trees have a hard time, actually, finding enough dirt to anchor their roots. They have the Ice Age to thank. Four distinct great glaciers gouged and plowed their way over this portion of the North American landscape, leaving virtually nothing except well-scoured rock to face the sun. It took about ten millenia to produce enough debris and humus to build these ten inches of soil to sustain the great forest.

The Canadian Shield dates back to the dawn of the Precambrian Era, which ended about 600 million years ago. The Shield is largely characterized by sudden steep precipices, massive boulders, and sharp ledges that either jut out from the banks of a stream or lie concealed just beneath the surface. Some of the rock, mostly granite, is 3.8 *billion* years old—so aged, in fact, that its birth was only a billion years or so after the earth was born. It is unquestionably the oldest rock on this continent.

On Burntside Lake near Ely, Minnesota, there is a point of land composed of rock more than 2.5 billion years old; it is greenstone, so called because of its dark green color. It's as compact and solid as only a permanent buttress of the planet can be. Originally formed from lava spewed forth from great fissures and fractures in the earth beneath the inland seas, greenstone is found in many areas of the North Woods. One stretch of it in Minnesota extends from the village of Tower through Ely to Moose Lake, a distance of some forty miles. In places it reaches 20,000 feet thick, a depth exceeding the tallest mountain on this continent.

The geological formation of the Shield, of course, is most interesting, but just as apparent in the landscape today are the monumental effects of the great glaciers that formed over it. Everywhere in the North Woods are marks left by the ice. Take for instance the Granite River, which has many islands and ledges that clearly show the planing and plucking action of the glaciers. Where the ice rode up on the rocks, they are polished smooth; at its source, where the glacier froze to the edge, the rock is broken and split, with missing chunks pirated by the ice as it moved onward, an inch, a foot, a yard a day. Along the Granite River, one can see much evidence of this evolutionary history; it is recorded in pebbles and boulders and scoured rock, all depicting the direction the ice went. In other places in the North Woods, the grooves and gouges are like the claw marks of some gigantic bear from a prehistoric time.

When I visited Burntside Lake, there in the ancient greenstone were the unmistakable markings, left some 15,000 years ago, of deep grooves cut by the rock-bearing glacier moving southward; higher up on the same point are boulders dropped from the same glacier as it retreated to the north, perhaps 2000 years later. These boulders are called erratics, for they were dropped at random upon the landscape.

During the Pleistocene spring the land was laid bare to the sun and the elements

Much of the Canadian Shield is barren rock; in other places the thin
soil supports scant vegetation, some of it considered old growth.

began to work upon it—sun, rain, snow, ice, and wind, and slowly, ever so slowly, insect and plant life began to appear. Clear lakes of meltwater with bottoms of granite pebbles and white quartz sand as pure as the water that covered it were everywhere. Boulders, pebbles, and chiprock formed integral parts of the landscape. Everywhere there was water; everywhere it was moving, making channels for the streams, outlets for the lakes, cascading down rapids and cataracts and waterfalls, curling through the valleys. In ten thousand years, it would become the North Woods across much of what today is Minnesota, eastern North Dakota, southern and central Manitoba, east-central Saskatchewan, western Ontario, and Michigan's Upper Peninsula. It was an evolutionary process; time would be needed for the creation. But all the ingredients were here for the great forest.

The Shield forms a sort of ellipse across the upper tier of the continent from the Atlantic to the Arctic Sea in the Northwest, and it underlies 1.8 million square miles of Canada and the Lake Superior and Adirondack regions of the United States. The North Woods, of course, do not extend to cover the entire Canadian Shield. But the boreal forest, sometimes—often—stunted beyond belief in more northern climes, does extend beyond the area generally thought of as the North Woods.

The largely conifer forest of the North Woods, one of three distinct great forest belts that girdle the North American continent, is sometimes called the boreal forest. It is so named in honor of Boreau, the Greek god of the north wind. The Russians call it the *taiga,* their word for the subarctic conifer belt in Siberia and northern Europe. While it is extensive in size, it is somewhat inferior in quality of growth, due to the thin soil and the long cold winter climate, which stymies growth for long periods of the year.

When some of these trees were in their infancy, the North Woods stretched across a great section of the continent, forming an immense dark roof of spruces and pines. Where the climax forest stood, trees as straight and tall as the columns of a Gothic cathedral rose to the heavens. About halfway up they branched out to form a canopy that the sun seldom penetrated. Consequently, the forest floor was a bed of soft pine needles; not much understory broke the vaulted chambers, so inviting to the first humans to walk among them.

Along streams and lakes in the damper areas of the forest grew stands of willow, aspen, and beautiful paperback birch, *Betula papyrifera.* It was from the latter that the first settlers, the Chippewa, and their ancestors some 8000 years previously, fashioned their birch-bark canoes. This craft, later adapted by the white man, would be the catalyst for opening up the North Woods.

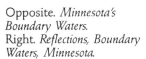

Opposite. *Minnesota's Boundary Waters.*
Right. *Reflections, Boundary Waters, Minnesota.*

The North Woods is, to put it simply, an infinity of trees. A few years ago when I flew out of Grand Marais on the north shore of Lake Superior to take a bird's eye view of some of the Quetico-Superior Wilderness, a part of which is now the Boundary Waters Canoe Area, I was impressed by the endlessness of it all. It seemed to stretch on forever. First of all, the Quetico-Superior Wilderness comprises some 16,000 square miles; 873,000-plus acres in the BWCA alone and another 1.15 million acres in the Quetico Provincial Park in western Ontario. Far more than that exists largely untouched and unprotected by law in Canada.

As impressive as the woodland was the water. Water was everywhere—mostly lakes and ponds, but also rushing streams that peeked occasionally through the dense canopy. The profusion of lakes alone was overwhelming. Manitoba claims 100,000, and a great many of those are in the North Woods region; Minnesota claims 10,000 on its auto license plate, but that actually is but a drop in the bucket compared to the actual number. Western Ontario has at least twice that many and maybe more. Looking at it from the air, it looked like an artist's canvas on which the gods had sprinkled drops of water that had miraculously expanded to become lakes and ponds.

Looking at it from a thousand feet up, it was some wonder to me that the French Voyageurs, without maps or compass, were able to find their way. It is even more wonder that modern-day canoeists do, even with modern charts and maps and all other kinds of navigational and landscape aids. For two hours our Cessna 182 roamed over the land and it seemed the farther we went, the more we saw of the same thing. It was an immovable landscape, strikingly impressive in the late August afternoon. A light haze hung over it, probably created by the trees themselves through transpiration. The blue of the waters bore sharp contrast to the lush green of this unforgettable forest.

Flying over this land brought memories of bygone years, when I had brought my small family up the Gunflint Trail in an old 1957 Volkswagen, carrying a pack of gear to rent a canoe and sample the Northern Light Lakes. Living in Louisville, Kentucky, at that time and working as a staff writer for United Press International, I didn't make enough money to take an expensive vacation. So my wife and I packed our two children into the back seat of the little car, threw all our camping gear on top and covered it with a tarp, and set out for a wonderful adventure. The VW was frugal on gas mileage, but we improved that by sticking close on the tails of semis traveling up busy Interstate 65 so the suction created by the big trucks literally pulled us along.

One year far back in the wilderness of the Quetico we encountered two canoeists whom I shall never forget. They were none other than naturalist and author Sigurd Olson and Supreme Court Justice William O. Douglas. The two men were close friends and upon several occasions had shared a canoe in the North Woods wilderness. My oldest son and daughter, David and Dianne, were very young at that time (four and two respectively) and they took noontime naps in the bottom of the canoe on seat cushions we placed there for them. Both men were obviously impressed that we would take children so young on adventures into the wild and told us so. We talked for an hour, perhaps, and I would have enjoyed their company on the entire ten-day trip. But they had been out for more than two weeks and were dead-heading for home. We had just begun to explore this wilderness, and we spent several nights huddled around a blazing fire on a lonely island listening to the forlorn

Clockwise from top left: *Loon and chick at Sylvania in Michigan's Upper Peninsula* (photo by John Ebeling). *Beaver building a lodge in the North Woods. Wild blueberries on the Canadian Shield of western Ontario. Timber wolf in the Quetico Wilderness of western Ontario* (photo by John Ebeling). *A black bear in the North Woods readies for the long winter's nap* (photo by John Ebeling).

Lake of the Clouds in the midst of Michigan's Porcupine Mountains.

call of loons far across the waters. It was an experience none of us ever forgot and often longed to repeat.

For some months after that expedition Justice Douglas and I corresponded upon several occasions, and somewhere I still have those handwritten notes. I admired both men until they died, and beyond, for they touched the spirit of many people during their own lives. America, in my estimation, never knew a finer pair of defenders of the natural environment; both wrote relentlessly and spoke endlessly on behalf of nature, and both adamantly loved the North Woods. Sigurd Olson, of course, lived most of his life in the North Woods at Ely.

The North Woods are mostly conifers. But they are dotted with hardwood forests at various pockets close to such boundaries as the Porcupine Mountains, along the southern shores of Lake Superior. The Woods are still today one of the continent's finest examples of old-growth forest, due to their vastness, the extensive waters which somewhat challenged logging operations, and because of the beaver. Yes, beaver.

Undoubtedly, there are more beaver in the North Woods than in any other location in the world. And there are far fewer beaver today than there were 200 to 300 years ago when logging was far more popular than it is today. There were so many beaver that anyone who came into the area thought of nothing else except trapping for pelts. They were much in demand in many parts of the world, especially in Europe. The Hudson Bay Company and the competitive Northwest Company, the latter absorbed in 1821 by the former, first traded with the Indians who trapped, then hired trappers and established villages deep in the frontier to exploit the beaver beyond the limits of the Indians who lived there.

The beaver pelts were carried by canoe all the way from the westernmost portions of the North Woods, a distance of nearly 2000 miles, to Montreal by the fun-loving, hard-working French Voyageurs. They were then shipped to England and other parts of Europe by the millions, mostly for clothing or living-quarters adornment. Before it was all over, the beaver population of the North Woods was practically eliminated. There were other fur-bearing animals in the North Woods, of course, as there still are today—black bear, cougar, mink, ermine, raccoon, fisher, and timber wolf—but it was the beaver that was popular during that time. Today they have come back in considerable numbers, but never to the extent they once were.

Another factor which has had a rather profound impact in parts of the North Woods is fire. Fire has always molded the land and all its life, and it has forever been an influence—for good or bad—in the forest. The North Woods are full of sharply defined demonstrations of fire's impact. Once it was thought that fire was only destructive to trees, but more recently ecologists have come to believe that fire contributes to the health and growth of a natural forest. In places, prescribed burns are planned by managers of forested areas. That is not the case in the North Woods, but it cannot be denied that fire does determine the basic character of any forest. Birch, jack pine, and aspen, while intolerant of fire, do seem to survive hardily through periodic ordeals, but fir and spruce have near-zero tolerance for fire. Many of the pines and hemlocks somewhat thrive on it. But, as Sigurd Olson said in his book *The Hidden Forest*, "only when fire is recognized as an ecological force with delicately interwoven relationships binding all living things to one another and to the earth, will we begin to understand its role."

The climate in the North Woods is ideal during the typically short summers—usually May is thaw-out time and October is freeze up, with occasional surprises on either end. The summers are generally cool, or if hot temperatures do occur, they're short-lived. Insects, particularly mosquitos and black flies, can be most bothersome. The winters are long and dark, with bitter cold and lots of snow and ice. Temperatures sometimes exceed -40° for days. Trees are sometimes threatened by ice buildups that weigh them down, break their boughs, and sometimes send them crashing to the ground.

The forest inhabitants, for the most part, sleep the long winters away. Many creatures migrate before winter comes sneaking down from the north; others merely dig burrows or slip underground to hibernate. In the more northern reaches of the North Woods, where it intertwines with the tundra area on the westernmost portions of Hudson Bay, the great white bear is in its heyday. It leaves the forest, where it spends much of the summer in search of a bare sustenance of berries and nuts, to hunt for seal on Hudson Bay after the freeze-up occurs. There is a general withdrawal and resting among the animal life in the frozen forest. The forest depends upon winter for fulfillment just as it depends on the warm-weather months for growth. Without the freezing process, certain spores, eggs, and seeds might not spring forth when the first warm days of spring knock on the forest door.

While the Quetico-Superior wilderness is indeed the largest remaining area representing the old-growth North Woods, there are others. The Menominee Indian Reservation in northeastern Wisconsin contains a very large block of old growth mixed pine and hardwoods, the largest single tract remaining in the Great Lakes states. The federal government prevented the Menominee from cutting their trees

Beautiful streams and waterfalls flow through the Porcupine Mountain Wilderness in Michigan.

during those decades when the forest fell everywhere else. Since the early part of the twentieth century, the Menominee have practiced a careful, selective cut, which has helped to conserve their homeland. So while it is not totally undisturbed, there are several thousand acres of old-growth trees still standing.

Protected pockets exist in other places, too, like McCarthy Beach State Park, twenty miles northwest of Hibbing, Minnesota, which has a fine stand of virgin pine on rolling hills between two lakes. There are also stands of virgin timber in the Flambeau State Forest and Chequamegon National Forest of Wisconsin. The town of Tomahawk, Wisconsin, has a 100-acre tract of virgin pine on the town's doorstep, preserved as a fine park. At Pine Grove Park near Little Falls, Minnesota, is an unusually fine example of virgin white pine, and near the town of Dora Lake in Cass County, Minnesota, is another outstanding tract.

In some places close to the perimeter of the North Woods, conifer forest such as Porcupine Mountains Wilderness State Park in Michigan's Upper Peninsula blends naturally with hardwoods. Here one will find white pine and red pine, fir and spruce standing alongside wild cherry, oak, maple, and hickory.

When I drove to Porcupine Mountains State Park on the south shore of Lake Superior that spring, I was surprised to see how many hardwoods there were, considering the harsh winter climate. The winter lasts as long as that of Hudson Bay; and in many ways, is just as severe. Great snows, sometimes exceeding 200 inches a year, lie on the ground from early November until late April, packing the woods like an iron blanket and often layered with ice.

But on the forest floor in July and early August was a profusion of little maple sprigs that appeared almost like ivy. I had never been to this area west of the Keweenaw on Michigan's Upper Peninsula during winter, and I don't anticipate going there again, but after I had settled my tent into a small grove of paperback birch trees

Opposite. A waterfall in the Porcupine Mountains.

at the Union River Campground, owner Norman Audette told me about the harsh winters. As early as November north winds begin piling up the ice on the south shore, sometimes building it in haystacks as far out on the lake as you can see. Ice caves form under it. The winds continue to blow across the ice, thoroughly chilling the land and the woods, covering the trees with brine frost at times, and piling the snow in deep drifts. It is beautiful, but the Audettes button up their place and migrate southward with the birds, all the way to south Florida, and they don't return until the spring thaw.

The campground is on the boundary of the state park and after a quick lunch I entered the park to explore some of the trails into its heartland. The park is larger than it might appear—65,000 acres—and it's sometimes called the crown jewel of Michigan's state park system. It is twenty-five miles long and ten miles thick at its widest point, with twenty-six miles of Lake Superior shoreline, four lakes (including the impressive Lake of the Clouds), numerous rivers, and waterfalls, and most of all, a dense old-growth forest that extends as far as the eye can see. Black bear, wolves, beaver, mink, porcupine, and a multitude of other animals roam its territory.

How it ever escaped cutting is somewhat a miracle. It came close. When copper mining started opening up on the Upper Peninsula, prospectors in 1845 opened the Union Mine on the east side of the park. It wasn't successful, however, and when it failed to show a profit, the owners sold it in 1864; finally it was abandoned altogether. Lumberjacks came to the Porkies, too, and cut a swatch close to the lake, but that is as much as they accomplished.

West of the Porcupines is an area I became acquainted with years ago while doing fishing stories for magazines in New York. It's called Sylvania and when I first began going there, it was still privately owned. President Eisenhower used to come there to fish for smallmouth bass and northern pike. My favorite experience in the North Woods occurred at Sylvania during the winter of 1967. Having tired of humdrum Christmases in the city (we then lived in Cincinnati), the family and I decided we would do something different. So we began making plans in October for a special Christmas in the North Woods.

I already had some idea of the harshness of the weather on the Upper Peninsula at that time of year, but it took courage to take my family along for a wilderness Christmas. Alan, our smallest, was just two years of age then, but spunky. We loaded up our El Dorado motorhome a few days before Christmas, including lots of "natural" decorations for the tree, packed the small closet with presents, and fashioned a special lock for it, just to keep the little peekers from being too nosy. Four days before Christmas, we motored up busy I-75 under a threatening sky.

It was snowing by the time we got into Michigan, and the farther we drove north, the heavier the snow became. Worse yet, it was sticking on the roads. We were forced to stop at a roadside rest stop to spend the night. The motorhome had a fine forced-air gas furnace and we all had excellent sleeping bags. It could sleep six and the two girls had chosen to stay with grandparents. So we had plenty of sleeping room.

The second day we made it all the way to the Straits at Mackinac Bridge that crossed over into the Upper Peninsula country. The winds and blowing snow were so gusty the bridge was closed. We spent a night in a supermarket parking lot—or

Overleaf left. *Old-growth paperback birch in the Porcupine Mountains.*
Overleaf right. *Along tiny brooks in the Porcupines only small trees can grow.*

most of the night. At 2 A.M., a snow plow operator awoke us to ask that we move to the other side of the lot so he could plow where we were. It was hard to sleep after we moved, and I listened to the wind howl, but in two hours it began to quiet and the skies began to clear. At 5 A.M. I drove across the bridge in the quiet deep freeze of the pre-dawn. Once on the north side, I turned west on US Highway 2. It was officially closed because of the blizzard, but I didn't know it. I drove all day. The road was now just the width of a cowpath. There was no other traffic, so I kept going. At 9 A.M. or so, the rest of the family rolled out of bed and had breakfast. I ate while driving. Periodic snowstorms, some nearly whiteouts, greeted us along the way. It was five to six feet in places. Anyway, we kept on, hardly able to tell the road from the snow-covered fields. No fences showed; the snow had risen above them.

By dark, we arrived at Watersmeet, a small town not far from the Wisconsin border and the center of Sylvania, the crown jewel of the Ottawa National Forest.

Sylvania ranger Marsh Lefler met me and guided us to a coveted spot in the old-growth forest. It was here we would camp the rest of the week. A new snowmobile with a pull-behind sleigh awaited; it was all we needed.

All around us were the great trees of this fine forest, their boughs gobbed with snow. Nearby was an eight-foot spruce just waiting to become our outdoor Christmas tree. We decorated it next day with strings of popcorn and cranberries, sugar cookies, shucked ears of Indian corn, and suet and other foodstuff for the birds and wildlife. This was our very first effort at what became an annual practice wherever we were at Christmas—a tree for the birds—and it was a ritual we continued for at least twenty years.

On Christmas morning, I had a surprise planned. I rode through the forest aboard the snowmobile in a Santa Claus suit I had purchased before leaving Cincinnati. Two of the younger children did not recognize me and little Alan was downright scared and crying. But the sight of a sleigh loaded with gifts helped to alleviate his fears of old St. Nick on a snowmobile.

The skies were clear, and the trees were popping like the sharp report of a gun from the bitter cold. It was just twenty below zero with forty-two inches of snow on the ground. But that was cold enough, and we certainly needed no more snow.

During the next few days, we lived in a winter heaven in the North Woods. Surely even the Voyageurs had never experienced such an adventure! We enjoyed every minute of this most unusual Christmas event. Over the next few days we ice fished, snowmobiled, snowshoed, and explored this winter wonderland—hemlocks burdened with snow, paperback birches, maples etched with crusty snow, and spruce. During that week, we photographed eight national magazine pieces on various subjects, including one about spending Christmas in the North Woods Wilderness. (People across America read about our Christmas there for a dozen years afterward. It became a perennial favorite.)

The North Woods old growth of Sylvania provided just the right setting; it was marvelous, and our adventure something to remember forever.

I did not return to Sylvania for more than twenty years. By that time it had changed considerably. A new visitors center had been built, trails constructed, ramps built on some of the lakes. But one thing had not changed—the great old trees that marked the centuries.

Sylvania had only been preserved as a prime example of North Woods old-growth forest because for many years it had been operated as a private hunt club. Otherwise, it would have been cleaned out of its treasures like most of the remainder of Michigan's Upper Peninsula.

Far to the south in the Wolverine State is another stand which came under state park protection—Hartwick Pines, just outside Grayling. It's as far south as any representative stand of the North Woods, but what a fine example it is. Although logging was conducted all around it, there are great white pines over 150 feet tall, some three to four feet in diameter at the base. Only forty-nine acres in size and containing a huge tree called the Monarch that dates back more than 300 years, this old-growth plot is part of a larger park containing 9762 acres. While the grove of white pine is by far the most impressive, there are also virgin jack pine and hemlock overlooking the broad valley of the AuSable River's East Branch.

Many years ago, I stopped there on a cold February day to photograph some winter scenes. There was not a soul in the park. Ten years later, I dropped by one

Far left. *Shelf fungus, Sylvania.*
Left. *Clark Lake at Sylvania in the Ottawa National Forest, Michigan's Upper Peninsula.*
Above. *Porcupine in the North Woods.* (photo by Denny Dumas)
Right. *Sylvania old growth.*

August Sunday and could hardly find a parking place. I was astounded that so many folks had come to appreciate old-growth forests, but my feelings were soon dispelled when I walked into the great piney woods. Only a half-dozen people strolled its trails. Tourists tinkered with their cameras and took pictures of each other in front of the big trees. Picknicking families and loud volleyball and softball games marred the fragile atmosphere.

I took a few pictures of the monumental trees and left. For me, the circuslike clamor was saddening. The terms old growth, silent sentinels, towering giants, monoliths—all began to take on new meaning. A thought flashed across my mind about the heavy hand of man and how little respect we hold for true values aside from ourselves. My one soothing thought existed in the knowledge that far away to the north across the Straits and Lake Superior there were still thousands of acres of wilderness, much of which had never recorded the footprint of man. There was at least some satisfaction in knowing that such a place existed—and would continue to exist—for many years to come in the North Woods.

FIVE

Forest of the Clouds

O n a rainy autumn day in 1991 I made my way down the winding road from Warren, Pennsylvania, along the Allegheny River. The broad leaves of the trees were tinted with suggestions of flamboyance yet to come. I carefully ridge-hopped southeast to a place fondly named Heart's Content. It wasn't a village, but an impressive grove of ancient Appalachian woods whose trees were already standing tall when George Washington commanded his ragged little army of revolutionaries across the Brandywine to fight a decisive battle against the British.

I parked, unloaded my camera gear, and then entered another world. I followed a trail that looped and dipped down the hillside past brooks and hideaways where deer and raccoon lurked a hundred generations before the Revolutionary War. The giant trees stood silent sentinels a good 200 feet over a forest floor draped with ferns and a veritable carpet of bunchberry and ground cedar. From somewhere within the hallowed recesses of this 121-acre remnant of old-growth wilderness echoed the lonesome call of a great pileated woodpecker. Here was a sanctuary of great vaulted chambers in which one could feel diminished to Lilliputian size and enlarged spiritually at the same time.

Towering black cherry, beech, white pine, and sugar maple mixed with ever-green virgin hemlock form the heart of this spared tract reaching upwards of 1800 feet above sea level. Only a hundred yards inside the chambered forest, I stood in awe. From the parking lot, located in an open grassy meadow, one has little indication that such magnificent old-growth monuments could exist barely a stone's throw away. But walking here was like entering through a veil that separated one world from another—the ordinary one out there which is real for most of us, and the most extraordinary one that now appeared almost a dream plucked from another era. I expected at any moment to see tiny trolls and leprechauns playing among the

Opposite. *A Smoky Mountain waterfall.*
Above. *Heart's Content, Pennsylvania.*

gardens of fern understory, or to meet face to face a tree called Moses. Yet all the time I fully realized no tree that old would be found here; it lived instead in the obscure fog-shrouded redwoods along the Pacific Coast or in the high Sierra Nevada sequoia groves nearly a continent away.

There was a damp softness in the forest air; light, filtered from the overcast skies through the dense canopy, projected an uncanny tone that caused every detail of the forest to shimmer. It was a marvelous effect, and a rare moment in time.

White pines and hemlocks born in centuries past provided a network of nurse logs from which hardy mushrooms and other fungus growth sprang. Here began the long process of chemically breaking down wood fiber and particles to be consumed by the new growth. From the time a tree dies, the invasion begins, creating a suitable habitat for ants, slugs, snails, earthworms, sawbugs, and an assortment of other insects. It is almost as though all these are part of the grand design. In time, the tree falls and thereby becomes more accessible to all the tiny creatures that live on or near the forest floor. The log becomes humus and returns to the soil to create food for other trees and animals. A chipmunk chattered excitedly nearby, telling me so.

The Alleghenies, which are a part of the greater Appalachians that extend all the way into Georgia and Alabama and link up with the Green and White Mountains of New England, push upward against the eastern shores of Lake Erie. Flying over this northwestern corner of the range on a clear day one can see all the way to the Great Smokies on the border of North Carolina and Tennessee, the highest mountains in this part of the country.

The Heart's Content area of the Alleghenies is but a few miles south of Lake Erie, a part of the St. Lawrence River watershed flowing northwestward into the North Atlantic. But this landscape drains instead into the Allegheny River, which joins the Monongahela coming out of the West Virginia high country to form the Ohio River at Pittsburgh. North of Lake Erie, the landscape is Canadian Shield country so sparsely vegetated that when French explorer Jacques Cartier first saw it in 1534, he muttered that "this must be the land God gave to Cain."

The Appalachian high country is neither barren nor bleak but covered in most places with great forests that grow fairly rapidly. The Heart's Content area is but a pinpoint on the map of old-growth forests, of course, but there are others, even in Pennsylvania, such as a large stand of virgin white pine in Cook Forest State Park.

Miles to the south, along U.S. 50 in West Virginia—the George Washington highway that runs coast to coast—is a grove of old growth, mostly hemlocks, that have been dear to me for many years. I have traveled that particular highway many times, and I never pass Cathedral State Park without pausing to pay homage to these giant trees. For thirty years, they have been old friends, and an enjoyable interlude in my travels. On summer days, there is always a refreshing, sweet breeze, and even in winter, I like to stop just to listen to the high mountain winds moan through them. In spring, the aroma of a forest awakening from the throes of winter is something I shall forever remember, and in fall, this mountain country is ablaze with the sunset hues of turning maple, beech, tulip poplar, dogwood, and sassafras, a carnival of color.

Cathedral State Park more resembled the redwoods of California than anything I had seen in the eastern portion of this continent. Every time I stopped to walk among these 400-year-old trees was a soul-lifting experience. The stand, of course, is small, with only a few dozen trees spared the saw and ax of an earlier era, but it is indeed enough to let one experience what all of this country in that part of the Appalachians was like 200 to 400 years ago.

Only a small number of places exist in the entire Appalachian chain to remind one of such an earlier era. There are still a few, thank goodness—Joyce Kilmer Memorial Forest in North Carolina; Lilley Cornett Woods and Beaver Creek in the Cumberlands of Kentucky; Linville Gorge in the Blue Ridge; and, of course, the greatest remaining old growth in the eastern United States, embodied within the confines of the Great Smokies National Park and straddling the lofty ridgetops of North Carolina and Tennessee.

The old Appalachians represent a most unusual geologic composite as well, and one that contributed greatly to the wide expanse of vegetation. Along the higher elevations is a forest that seems ill-placed in these latitudes; it seems to belong instead in the northern reaches of Canada. In a range of only a few hundred miles, one may experience the kinds of forest embodied in north to south regions of the entire eastern part of the continent.

The Smokies are the highest mountains in the Appalachian chain, with sixteen

The Great Smoky Mountain National Park.

peaks rising above 6000 feet elevation. For almost thirty-four miles the crest of this part of the Appalachians does not dip below 5000 feet, nor is it crossed by a single stream. Here there are no bare peaks, although they do occur in other parts of the Appalachians. This is because they were never glaciated, so the soil was not removed or scraped away in the higher elevations.

When the glaciers traveled south—and there were four distinct epochs, each lasting hundreds of thousands of years—they leveled many land forms ahead of them all the way to the Ohio River Valley and what was once the ancient Teays. They changed not only the land form, but vegetation and wildlife as well. Creatures and plants that normally lived elsewhere were pushed southward, to either adapt to the new environment created beyond the thick tongues of the glaciers or to perish. This

Opposite. *Autumn brings out the old-growth diversity of the Smokies. Clockwise from above: Dogwood trees color the mountains during late April and early May. Winter in the Smokies. Rhododendron. Turkey vultures rest in a dead tree, Cornett Woods, Kentucky.*

is claimed to be a major reason for the vast array of botanical growth in the Smokies area, including the greatest accumulations of wildflowers found anywhere in this entire hemisphere. Today there are 1400 species of flowering plants, 325 mosses and liverworts, and 1200 fungi.

Never in geological history has a single event caused greater change—change which remains so evident to this day in botanical growth. As a result, here may be found plant and animal life from the south and north and from lower and higher elevations. When the noted naturalist William Bartram traveled through the Smokies in 1775—the first botanist to visit the area—he could not believe his own findings. He indicated it to be the most diverse and interesting botanical area he had ever experienced and once told a Cherokee Indian friend he would be most content to spend the rest of his life here.

I once hiked with another friend, Woody Landers of Pigeon Forge, Tennessee, along a section of the 2000-mile Appalachian Trail that wends its way along much of the crest of these mountains. He was impressed with the area, too: trudging up an 8 percent grade that would get steeper in places, Woody paused to get his breath and exclaimed, "God, these mountains are older than Methuselah." The fact is, they are eons older than Methuselah or anyone else on earth at any time.

Noticeable by their absence are any fossils in the rocks. These geological formations, created more than 500 million years ago, were formed before life was abundant on the planet. They were uplifted with awesome geological force to an elevation higher than the Alps. In this Oconee series, as they are referred to by scientists, the rains and winds and snows have worn them down to the stage you see them today, with rounded tops and only a few instances of craggy pinnacles.

From the tops of the crests, the Smokies and neighboring Blue Ridge in particular appear as layered mountains, one range stacked against another. The haze created by distance, and the different shades of color corresponding with the variations, led to their names. This division was later broken down to give greater definition to the complex belt rising more than 3000 feet above sea level. In the Blue Ridge, Grandfather Mountain (5964 feet), Standing Indian, (5562 feet) and Pinnacle (5665 feet) were impressive enough, but just fifty miles west near the borders of Tennessee, Virginia, and Kentucky—where Daniel Boone found a way west to the new lands—the massive Unaka area sports eighteen peaks rising above 5000 feet. This area, sculpted by such scenic rivers as the Little Tennessee, Pigeon, French Broad, Nolichucky, and Hiwassee, includes such segments as the Great Smokies, Unicoi, Bald, and Northern Unaka.

Throughout this particular area are vestigial bridges and cross-ranges of land. This was brought dramatically to mind one January not long ago as I boarded a jetliner and soared some 38,000 feet on a diagonal path over the Blue Ridge. Unfolding before the eye at this elevation was a panorama I shall never forget—a huge relief map which allowed me to view in great detail the whole of the Smokies and most of the Blue Ridge. Most of man's irritating alterations disappeared entirely from view in the early-morning light. It was almost as though I was seeing the Appalachians as they might have appeared 500 or 1000 years past.

I thought about all the great forests down there, but from this godlike point of view, it was insignificant. Only when I hiked through portions of them would the great trees take on the magnitude that would cause me to stop often and stand in awe, getting cricks in my neck from looking skyward. And when I trudged along the Appalachian Trail with Woody, I found myself thinking of that vast prehistoric-appearing landscape that in one quick glance encompassed an area the best of hikers would take several weeks to traverse.

Woody and I, like so many nature lovers, had come to the high country to find that special alpine experience of solitude and wilderness. But we had not gone more than five miles before we realized the Appalachian Trail, instead of wilderness, was not unlike a major highway—only here the travelers were on foot. There were many of them, and during this and subsequent visits to various segments of the Appalachian Trail, I found myself lamenting the overuse and abuse along the trail, simply from so many of those wonderful cleated hiking boots traveling this way. The great trees—what there were left of them in places—suffered from skeleton roots exposed like octopus arms on top of the ground, packed and worn away by the many hikers. In places, the trail was badly eroded. I thought of William Bartram and how wonderful it must have been to hike for a whole week or two without encountering another person and even then only an Indian or two, perhaps themselves seeking solitude.

But the Smokies are a wonderful place; there are some recesses in these mountains where one can find a true wilderness experience. "This park," botanist Keith Langdon assured me on my last visit, "has 70 percent old-growth forest..." He paused, staring at the ceiling of his office. "Of course, that depends upon your definition of old growth. A lot of the trees we consider old growth may be no more than 100 to 150 years old. They are located at higher elevations, where trees just don't grow very old because of the elements, the harsh climate, the thin soils. They die young, so to speak, and not from any influences of man necessarily. But in other areas we have trees 400 years old."

Some years previously, I had worked on a *National Geographic* project on the old-growth forests of the Smokies. I had packed my camera gear into some impressive high territory called the Greenbriar and Ramsey Cascade, which supported big, big trees—oak, maple, wild cherry, hickory, hemlock, and a multitude of others. I had been told then that these areas were the finest old-growth forests in the entire Smokies. In my estimation, they still are, filled with giants up to four feet or more in diameter and 200 feet tall. It was spring when I was first there and winter winds still moaned through the barren canopy, where only a few buds had reacted to moments of sun. The understory of the forest was yet to come—ferns were breaking through a crust of winter leaves as fiddleheads and early mushrooms peeked through the thin soil. A few trilliums poked their heads up, and violets and dwarf wild irises were already in bloom. In a few weeks, it would turn into a veritable flower garden.

"Old growth." Langdon scowled at the ceiling again. "It's short-lived, you know. The big trees are in trouble. Seems they have a lot more odds against their safe survival now than ever before. The gypsy moth, which has plagued much of New England and the Mid-Atlantic forests, is headed this way. In fact, we've already had a couple of small outbreaks in the park this year. It's 1991 now...who knows what kind of a forest we'll have in ten years if they infest this area? There are threats from other types of critters, too. So what man did not destroy before this became a park in

A Greenbriar cliff.

1934, he may destroy through exotics he has since introduced into the country. It might be the final curtain call for the rest of it."

Nonetheless, at this point, the Smokies are indeed one of the finest large-scale examples of remaining old-growth forests in eastern America. Of the 800 square miles of area in the park, 160,000 acres is considered virgin. It is one of America's most popular parks, partially due to its proximity to great population centers, but if one takes the time and makes the effort to get away from the main thoroughfares, one can indeed find impressive remnants of The Forest Primeval. In some cases, I've waded raging boulder-strewn streams, risking broken bones or being washed away, in order to find solitude. Once found, I'm as protective of it as a mother wolf of her pups. Occasionally, while teaching a nature photography workshop in the Smokies, I take my students to a fairly remote grove of old-growth hemlocks just to give them the opportunity of experiencing such a primeval forest. In this particular grove is a small brook with steppe waterfalls cascading down the side of the mountain. One fall in particular is most photogenic from a large flat rock jutting over the stream.

On one occasion, a middle-aged couple was already perched on the rock as I marched my class, one by one, onto it to photograph the stream. After the fifth or sixth student, the man got up and came over to me, scowling.

Grottos of icicles in the Appalachian high country.

"Who's in charge of this group?" he asked.

"I am."

"Sir," he fumed, "my wife and I searched this place out in order that we might enjoy it in some solitude. We do not appreciate you bringing your class to interfere with our peace."

At first, I was a bit dumbfounded, but I quickly recovered.

"But sir," I answered, "I bring my class to this particular spot every year—have been for ten years or more. We reserve this section of stream every year at this time for my class to photograph. Did you check with the ranger?"

He stood staring at me, still scowling. Then he turned, helped his wife to her feet, and off they rushed down the trail. To this day, I wonder if he ever learned that I had fed him a story. I think even some of my class believed I actually had reserved this remote spot in the woodlands.

In certain areas, like the Greenbriar, the big trees area is treated as true wilderness. As I once hiked into that area, I came upon a Park Service crew clearing a tree which had fallen across the trail. No loud raucous whine of a chain saw echoed through these woods; instead, the ring of a broadax and the seesaw grind of a hand-operated crosscut saw, the kind I had been accused by my father of riding when I was

Opposite. *A community of spiderwebs in Heart's Content.*
Above. *Grey fox, Cornett Woods.*
Left. *Beech leaves in autumn, Cornett Woods.*
Below. *Dwarf iris.*

a small boy in our own Kentucky woodland. Only hand-operated tools could be used in this area, I was told, in keeping with the Park Service's policy on maintaining a wilderness atmosphere.

Other old-growth forests such as the mountain grove just above the Chimneys Picnic Area or the area back of Laurel Falls are easier to reach. I particularly like the area back of Laurel Falls, although, for the life of me, the hike to the falls seems to stretch every year. I never go there that I'm not reminded of an experience one April while working on a magazine project some years ago. The woods were sultry on this particular day, and by late morning a sudden electrically charged mountain storm rushed across the land with little advance warning. Having packed my camera gear in, I had no way of keeping it dry, so I ducked under a rocky outcrop to protect it. Hardly had I settled in away from the downpour, as lightning bounced off the ground outside, than I became aware I wasn't alone.

Looking about in the semidarkness, I finally made out the beautiful coppertone sheen of a snake no more than three feet away. It was a beautiful specimen of a copperhead, one of the most plentiful toxic reptiles in the Smokies. It had not moved, but lay there peering as much at me as I was at it and perhaps wondering the reason for this intrusion.

I looked carefully about but saw no others, for I knew sometimes where there is one, there are two or more. It could have been the lair for a whole family. If it was, I saw no more. Both it and I waited out the storm silently, although I may have actually spoken a greeting or two to it during the interlude. But once the storm had passed, I quickly departed, leaving my companion to its own pleasure.

Without question, the Smokies are the centerpiece for old growth in the Appalachians. No other place offers the variety or vastness of these woods. True, there are others like Heart's Content of the Alleghenies; Huntington Wildlife Forest

Wild Woodlands

of the Adirondacks, with more than a thousand acres of sugar maple, yellow birch, and red spruce; Plateau Mountain in the Catskills; Linville Gorge in North Carolina, which was blazing with flaming azalea when I visited it; and Joyce Kilmer, on the doorstep of the Smokies. But none of these measures up to the Smokies.

I simply love Joyce Kilmer Memorial Forest in the Nantahala National Forest, but for some strange reason every time I've gone there, I encounter a downpour. Comprising some 3800 acres of wilderness, it embodies sizable sections of old growth and some of the finest natural forest atmosphere in the East.

But so does Linville Gorge, which has some one hundred acres of giant hemlock, claimed to be the largest stand of virgin hemlock in the eastern United States.

It is befitting and proper that the Joyce Kilmer Memorial Forest should be named after this journalist who once was on the staff of *The New York Times*, but who made his niche in literary history with a simple poem—"Trees"—once memorized by every schoolchild in America. It reads:

> I think I shall never see
> A poem lovely as a tree.
>
> A tree whose hungry mouth is prest
> Against the earth's sweet flowing breast;
>
> A tree that looks at God all day
> And lifts her leafy arms to pray;
>
> A tree that may in Summer wear,
> A nest of robins in her hair;
>
> Upon whose bosom snow has lain;
> Who intimately lives with rain.
>
> Poems are made by fools like me,
> But only God can make a tree.

The Joyce Kilmer Forest is one of America's most impressive examples of wilderness.

The trees of the Smokies and Joyce Kilmer were spared simply because time ran out for exploitation, but over in the Cumberlands of Kentucky, another factor saved the Beaver Creek Wilderness in the Daniel Boone National Forest. Here it was the geography and geology of the place that made the difference. Consisting of some 5000 acres, Beaver Creek Woods is located in a scenic sunken canyon surrounded by large sandstone cliffs. Rock houses and shallow caves pockmark the cliffs, which are nearly 200 to 400 feet high.

Made up of mixed pine, hemlock, maple, elm, ash, yellow poplar, and various oaks and hickories, and with an understory of mountain laurel and rhododendron, this forest simply was too difficult to get to in the early days when forests were being cut in this section. So it was bypassed. By the time later methods were developed to hoist the logs out of the canyon, a move was afoot to save it for posterity.

Not so far away as the crow flies in the Cumberlands, however, is perhaps the most affecting story of all, the story of one man's love affair with a forest. Lilley Cornett, a coal miner, shortly after World War I purchased the first of five tracts that now make up one of the finest mixed mesophytic forest in all the Cumberlands. Lilley Cornett Woods represents the best development of such a forest anywhere.

108

A rainy summer day along a stream in Joyce Kilmer Memorial Forest, North Carolina.

Top. *Grayback stone that tumbled from the high country centuries ago.*
Left. *Turkey tail fungus.*
Above. *A mother mallard ushers her ducklings along the west fork of the Little Pigeon.*

An amanita mushroom, sometimes referred to as "the angel of death," an apt designation. Beaver Creek Wilderness, Kentucky.

Having saved his money over a period of years, Cornett was able to buy the forest piecemeal. Later he hired others in the neighborhood to help him fight fires and post security. For years he fought off offers by timber barons to buy up the trees and cut down the woods. He allowed not one living tree to be cut. Cornett so loved his woods that when he died, his devotion was passed on to his children who, like their father, refused offers for the timber. Instead, they tried to find some institution that would help protect the forest for future generations. In July of 1969, the University of Kentucky and Eastern Kentucky University took over the responsibility of management and protection. Now that forest is used for advanced ecological research and instruction in related college-level courses. Lilley Cornett would be proud.

The remaining great old-growth forests of the eastern mountains are indeed a study not only in forest types, but other more romantic qualities: the soft pale greens on early spring and summer mornings, the sounds of bubbling brooks and rushing rivers, the silence of vaulted forest chambers where a prothonotary warbler breaks the stillness in song or where a winter snowflake alights with a quiet flair all its own. These woods are distinctive, subtle, filled with solitude. As Mike Frome, author of a fine book called *Strangers in High Places*, wrote of the Smokies some years ago: "Happily, in a world where nothing remains static, the Great Smoky Mountains provide the prescription to ward off ills and evils born of super-civilization." It's something that applies to every remnant of old-growth forest in the Appalachians.

SIX

The Heartlands

When I was a child, I would spend hours sitting with my back against a great oak tree in our farm woodlands in Kentucky dreaming of the great forests that once covered this land. Much of the Midwest was once wooded with great stands of mixed mesophytic forest—oak, hickory, beech, cherry, poplar, and sassafras. Wild grapevines as big around as a man's leg tied them together.

Some of the trees in our twenty-acre woodlot seemed a lot bigger to me then than they would now. But I am not sure, for when I was in high school my father sold all the biggest trees to a logger who came in and cleared them out. I never forgave my father for that act. The money was not needed, just another crop to be harvested. The trees were ready to be cut, he said.

I don't ever recall any indication—and I spent a lot more time with the trees than did my father   that they were ready to be cut down. They seemed content in the playful breezes and warm summer rains. I can recall walking among them in late fall as the final leaves came spinning or wafting to the ground. And I can remember walking among them as it began to snow, feeling the big wet flakes settle upon my face as I closed my eyes and looked up. The flakes would melt and snow tears would form in the crevices of my ears and in the corners of my eyes until I wiped them away. It was a great feeling.

Redtail hawks and owls would scold me from their lofty perches among the treetops. Bluejays and blackbirds—whole flocks of blackbirds—would gather on their way south and their noisy chirps would literally fill the air. Woodpeckers drummed in the distance on hollow snags. A thousand and one tiny creatures all lived here—worms, moths, snakes, lizards, a hundred different kinds of bugs. Squirrels were plentiful in years we could keep out the hunters, and there was cottontail rabbit, fox, skunk, raccoon, opossum—a marvelous community of all kinds of life. It

Opposite. *Old-growth and new-growth maple, Beall Woods.*

Above. *Chipmunk in Hoot Woods.*
Left. *Luna moth, Dysart Woods, Ohio.*

was always a fascinating place to be and to spend hour after hour just wandering about or sitting on a log thinking.

No, this was not an old-growth forest by any means, but in my mind's eye at age eleven it was old enough. In another thirty years I would finally get to know some real old-growth forests with ancient trees older than this nation. In the heartlands, too, which is about the last place in America one would expect to find old-growth forest.

After I had begun to make a name for myself in the publishing world, I developed friendships in the national and state offices of The Nature Conservancy, an organization with whom I was most impressed. I agreed with the good conservation work they did, much of it without acclaim or fanfare. And periodically, because I could now have some impact through my work, they would call upon me to take a look at certain natural areas which they hoped to purchase for preservation. One of these was a forty-acre old-growth forest in Indiana, where I lived at that time, called Hoot Woods. It was so called because it was part of a larger farm tract owned by elderly sisters of the name Hoot.

Some scientific studies had already been made public on the tract and the

114

results were quite impressive. Many of the large trees here exceeded 150 years, which at that time preceded the settlement of the Hoosier State. Hoot Woods is predominantly huge beeches, some of them measuring nearly four feet in diameter. Several white oaks are nearly as big, and there are large numbers of great sugar maple, poplar, white ash, red elm, black cherry, red ash, yellow or chinquapin oak, black gum, white oak, and shagbark hickory.

It was a lazy autumn day when I knocked upon the door of the Hoot sisters' simple frame farmhouse. The farm, located near the town of Freedom, had been in the family for generations, and Alice Hoot and her sister, Dorothy, were at that moment determined to keep it that way. I was welcome to take a stroll through the woods with my cameras on this particular October day, however, and so I did. It was sunny but windy—too windy to be at ease in the woods. Dead limbs kept dropping down about me, and one narrowly missed me. I hadn't brought along a hard hat. But it was certainly an impressive and unforgettable visit. The beech and maples were ablaze with color, as were some of the oaks. Yellows and golds were predominant, but there was a fair mixture of reds and ambers as well. It was a rare experience in living color.

A week later, I was in another Indiana old-growth forest less than forty miles away as the crow flies. Donaldson Woods at Spring Mill State Park on the doorstep of Mitchell, the late astronaut Gus Grissom's hometown, is somewhat the same type of forest, but here the beech is not the predominant tree. White oaks and wild black cherry and poplar mainly make up this forest.

Donaldson Woods had lost most of its fall foliage already but its great white oaks stood straight and tall, with a fine-meshed bark that gave them their name. I had always loved white oaks from my growing-up days on the farm. We had a number of them, ranging up to three feet in diameter, and I learned then to appreciate the feel of their bark. It was rough, but not nearly as rough as the great red oaks or shagbark hickories. It was hard and did not crumble, and while it had texture, it was not a rough texture. So naturally, when I came to Donaldson Woods, I photographed the white oaks, but not before feeling them. There was something very therapeutic about feeling the trees. I sometimes would play a game: by closing my eyes in the woods and feeling my way with my toes, I would make my way from tree to tree, feeling them and stroking them with my hands and trying to identify each one.

Every tree was different, some of them radically so. A red oak's rough black bark (I never did figure out why they are called red oaks, when their bark is distinctly black) was dirty. It crumbled in your hands and the black residue was hard to rub off. The shagbark was so rough with its sharp edges on the curled-up bark that it would either break off or threaten to cut your skin. Not a pleasant tree to feel. To touch a beech is perhaps the most sensuous experience of all. Let's face it—these are sexy trees. It's on beeches you're most likely to find lovers' initials carved. The bark is exceedingly smooth and you have to practice a good deal of self-discipline when stroking a beech tree. It's even hard to keep your eyes closed.

I did not intend to get carried away with the feel of trees, but Donaldson Woods, where a great variety of trees live, is as good a place as any to think about feeling trees with your eyes closed. Just don't let the park rangers see you.

Donaldson Woods is impressive, but there's another old-growth forest over on the Wabash River where it divides Illinois and Indiana which is even more so. It's

Donaldson Woods in January.

called Beall Woods, now a state park devoted mostly to the forest environment. The soils traditionally are far more fertile along the lower Wabash than in the rolling hills of Spring Mill State Park. Consequently, trees which may be no older than those at the Spring Mill here could be a third larger simply because of more nutrients and lots of water, sometimes from the flooding stream.

So though you might find a white oak in Donaldson Woods that is three feet thick at the base, over in Beall Woods on the Wabash a tree of the same age might be close to four feet across at the base. The growth rings will just be farther apart.

Beall Woods is the only place I've ever visited where the park naturalist recommended I wear a hard hat for safety reasons. During late summer and autumn, because of walnuts, hickory nuts, and even acorns of unusual size plummeting from the trees, it's certainly advisable, to avoid the risk of being hurt.

Donaldson Woods, Spring Mill State Park, Indiana.

One of the most impressive old-growth forests in the entire Midwest also is located in southern Indiana, but it's unbelievably small—no more than ten acres. Located at a roadside rest stop near Paoli, sixty miles west of Louisville, Kentucky, it's called Pioneer Mother's Wayside Memorial, a natural old-growth stand of black walnut and other trees. The walnuts tower above the forest floor, and it's a wonder they're still standing, considering the high price of walnut. To walk the narrow dirt trail leading through the grove is an experience not to be missed. The best time, of course, to go there is during the warm weather months.

Most Midwestern states are totally devoid of old-growth forests, but pockets do remain in some of them. A small privately owned tract is located on the Wisconsin River near Tomahawk, Wisconsin; an old man in his eighties lives there and controls its fate. And in Ohio, which was once virtually covered with fine old-growth forest, is

Clockwise from right:
Maple leaves in October.
Zebra swallowtail butterfly,
Beall Woods. Hornet's nest in
the autumn woods.

Above. *A grey fox at the edge of a meadow clearing in Donaldson Woods.*
Below left. *Dogwood.* Below right. *Patterns in bark of an ancient beech tree.*

Whitetail deer fawn.   *Toxic copperhead snake.*

Dysart Woods, now owned by Ohio University at Athens. Located in Belmont County in the southeastern part of the Buckeye State, it is considered a rare fragment of primeval virgin forest, with white oak and tulip poplars twelve feet around rising some one hundred feet above the forest floor. These woods have been called the finest oak-hickory forest between the Atlantic Ocean and Indiana.

In Missouri, there are several old-growth woods still remaining, but only in smaller tracts. Among them is Big Oak Tree State Park close to the Mississippi River. Although there are only about sixty acres in the entire park, it does include a world champion persimmon tree. At Van Meter State Park located in the Missouri River hills of Saline County is a mixed oak-hickory forest with some very outstanding black walnut. And in the White River country of southwest Missouri is an eastern red cedar and ash juniper stand with some trees more than 400 years old. Called the Ashe Juniper Natural Area, it is located close to the city of Springfield. Most of the old-growth forests remaining in the Heartlands are the result of families that owned and maintained them as natural areas for years, sometimes generations, before finally relinquishing them to either The Nature Conservancy or to state park systems to be preserved for posterity.

Few people living in the Heartlands today, of course, realize the magnitude and importance of the vast forests that once covered most of the Midwest. Ohio, Indiana, Wisconsin, Missouri, and parts of Illinois were one great forest. A squirrel 400 years ago could actually travel from the banks of the Delaware to the Mississippi without ever touching ground. He couldn't do that today, and we are the poorer for it.

Opposite. Donaldson Woods, Spring Hill State Park, Indiana.

The Saguaro National Monument near Tucson, Arizona.

SEVEN

The Desert Forest

As far as the eye could see there lay the desert. From this observation platform at the Sonoran Desert Museum west of Tucson, it shimmered in the thermals of spring. I had never seen this desert before, and I stood in awe at the austere beauty of it. It was hotter than I had expected this early in the year. It was April, and the landscape was in full bloom.

The Arizona-Sonoran Desert, named after two states, one American, one Mexican, is often referred to as the most unusually interesting desert in this hemisphere, if not the world. No question about it—this desert is unique, and largely because of the great diversity of plant and animal life that calls this expanse of the planet, extending from southern Arizona well into the state of Sonora in Old Mexico, home. Covering some 119,000 square miles, it actually embodies 2360 miles of seacoast along the Gulf of California—longer than the American Pacific doorstep.

One of its greatest natural assets is the vast forest that covers some sections of this desert. It is filled with the giant saguaro, a tree cactus with wooden ribs that may grow up to sixty feet or more. (Some claims have been as high as eighty feet, but no official measurements have documented such heights.)

While there are other trees in the southwest desert forest—the Joshua tree, found in the Mojave, the almost leafless paloverde, which often serves as a nurse tree to the saguaros, and the organ pipe cactus—it is perhaps the saguaro more than any other which symbolizes the great Southwest. The great saguaro has character and it attracts lots of attention. It symbolizes space, the old West of gunslinger days, the coyote and the cowboy, the pistol, the lariat, and even the sun. "When you see a saguaro," John Wayne, who loved the Sonoran Desert, once said, "you only have to use a little imagination to see the whole of the Southwest in the mind's eye. The saguaro is everything."

Although they are in some ways intimidating, and covered with thorny spines that hurt upon contact with the skin, they can also be as loveable as any other tree. While their age seldom extends more than 200 years and more likely 150, the saguaros in many ways encompass the same ageless quality as the California redwoods or the giant sequoias. There is something grand and noble about them.

On that first visit in 1976 to the great southwest desert country, I immediately fell in love with the saguaros. I have returned there a score or more times, and have spent up to a month or more there, and I am as much in love with them today as I was when introduced. I don't think the love affair will ever cease.

When one of the grandfather saguaros I came to know in subsequent years began to die, I was likely the only one who lamented its demise. Every year, I made devoted pilgrimages to its side and stood gawking up at its mighty arms like some small child who had never see a saguaro before. I imagined all the history that had lapsed—especially in my own life—during the time span this old cactus had been living. Some years later, after I began to teach nature photography workshops in the desert southwest, I took my students to visit this old friend. Its long curling arms embraced the desert sky, and as the long-term illness and aging persisted, it had rested its broken, heavier ones upon the earth. Still, it continued to blossom for some years after I came to know it. Each May and June, lovely wax-white lilylike clusters of flowers crowned the tips of the healthier arms. As the years passed, however, it ceased to blossom anymore and finally, entire arms began falling to the ground, broken and torn away from the main body.

Each year when I left I knew this might be the final time I would see it alive. But it happened more suddenly than I expected. For several years, the demise had been gradual. But when I returned one year, I found absolutely nothing. There was not even the slightest sign this saguaro had ever existed. I searched and probed in the desert floor where I was almost certain it had stood. But the desert had already covered up whatever remains there had been. Apparently, I reasoned, it had fallen and, existing too close to a passing road, someone had taken the wooden ribs for firewood. The skin had dried like pieces of old leather and the hot winds and rains during the desert monsoon season had cleaned away the rest.

At first I could not believe my eyes. I even doubted my own sanity. Had I imagined the great saguaro? Had I imagined even coming here year after year to visit it? When I returned home I searched through the many pictures I had taken of it. No, the camera had not lied. The great saguaro had indeed lived and blossomed year after year, had felt the boiling desert sun and the infrequent rains and the soft breezes that blew down from Telescope Mountain. It may even have seen my small group of nature-loving students accompany me to its base time after time to record its beauty upon film. It was not, after all, a figment of my own imagination. It really had stood there, maybe for nearly two centuries, since it was sprouted from a tiny wind-blown seed carried from another saguaro. Now it was gone forever, of course, but it would live on and on for many years yet to come, through my own memory and the memories of the hundred or so students I had shared it with over a ten-year period.

Over the years I was to enjoy many experiences and encounters with the Sonoran Desert and the saguaro in particular. I came to learn more and more about them through friends who were researchers and botanists, plus my own reading.

A Boojum Tree standing beside a saguaro in the Sonoran Desert;
these are normally found in the Mexican forest, but only
occasionally in Arizona.

Claret cup cactus.

Teddy Bear cactus in the desert forest of southwest Arizona.

A summer tanager.

Chuckwallas live around rocky areas in the Sonoran Desert and may be found in communities.

From the beginning, I had come to respect and admire these great tree cactus for their size, age, and simple beauty.

I remember being caught in a flash flood some years ago as I was doing field work for one of my books. I was parked in the downpour near a desert wash not far from Tucson. The rain came down in sheets and within forty-five minutes the desert became a lake. Everywhere I looked was water. It was no more than a foot deep, perhaps only inches, but the dry wash nearby became a roaring stream from which emerged snakes, lizards, and other creatures bent upon survival. The great saguaros which stood sparsely around me began to swell before my eyes. Their rib-accordion structures began to expand, and I knew the water was being soaked up by the expansive root system. I returned the next day just out of curiosity; the saguaros were perhaps a third larger than they had been prior to the rain. (In some cases, they may expand their girth as much as 50 percent during a single rainstorm.)

I was fascinated. Later, I learned even more about the saguaros. They actually may weigh up to seven or eight tons, of which water constitutes 75 percent or more. By storing up all this moisture, the saguaro can then live for up to two years without another drop of rain. During the course of its lifetime, a saguaro may bear as many as fifty million seeds, but only *three or four* of these may survive to maturity. This high mortality rate is easily explained: everybody likes them. Ground squirrels, ants, white-winged doves, coyotes, and even the Indians love the sweet, succulent fruit.

Green fruit, the size of a child's fist, develops after flowering and pollination in late May or June. It continues to mature in the superheated and desiccated desert, a place where it is hard to imagine how anything can live even another day. But it does. Finally, in late June or early July, when it has not rained for perhaps a hundred days,

In rocky areas of the Arizona-Sonoran Desert are found endangered desert bighorn sheep such as this old buck.

when the brittlebush has been reduced to a haphazard collection of withered stems and crumpled, gray leaves, the saguaro fruits restore hope and color to the desert as they turn pale orange or red. Then they swell and split, exposing a brilliant crimson interior that frames a sticky mass of black seeds set in a sweet, moist matrix. They're a nutritious, high-calorie, high-protein food devoured by all kinds of desert creatures, from jawed long-horn beetles to house finches.

Even the saguaro's cooling system is remarkable. The long clusters of thorns adorning its accordion-rib structure not only serve to protect it from predators, but they act as a cooling device, similar to an air-cooled engine. The surface of the thorns is cooled by the air passing over them; this coolness is transmitted through the leatherlike surface, thereby maintaining interior temperatures that are one-third cooler than they might otherwise be.

So it is with great admiration, respect, and awe that I stand beneath this king of the cacti. The whole cacti community is fascinating and old, dating back some 20,000 years. But the saguaro, in part because of its size, is exceptional.

Since my introduction to the saguaro in the Saguaro National Monument, I have expanded my intimacy upon several occasions. I seldom visit Phoenix that I do not escape to the little community of Cave Creek, where I drive eight or ten miles down a jeep trail leading into the Tonto National Forest. There the rocky mountain slopes that drop to the creek are covered with a large population of saguaros. The forest is quiet, and the creek and its narrow valley virtually undisturbed by other human beings on weekdays. I choose my way carefully and slowly along the rugged road, which enters the creek several times and emerges in the dusty desert beyond.

The creek is crystal clear, and periodically along its banks are grassy level plots that serve as excellent campsites. A quick dip into the cool waters alone is worth the rugged trip.

From my camp alongside the bubbling stream, I often hike among the saguaros, exploring the solitude of this secluded off-the-beaten-path place. I like best to walk among them on moonlit nights, watching bats flitting and listening to the lonesome wail of a pack of coyotes. Several times over a period of years I was visited in my camp by a white horse, its mane matted with cockleburs. Sometime later, I met its owner in Cave Creek, who informed me that the horse was "old Ben Cartwright's horse from *Bonanza.*" It had been retired and released to green pastures among the saguaros. Apparently lonely and eager to visit again with humans, it came to my camp to stay a good many nights. It would be there when I bade the saguaros good night and it would be there when I arose at the first hint of day—meetings I will never forget.

The saguaro is indeed a great symbol of the American Southwest. No other is quite as evocative, even though its true range is pretty well confined to that part of the Sonoran Desert east of the Colorado River and south into the upper reaches of the Mexican state of Sonora. Northward, the saguaro lives in protected areas of desert mountains and canyon country almost to Flagstaff and the San Francisco Peaks. But its greatest stands are found in the Saguaro National Monument around Tucson.

Like almost everything else constituting our natural environment these days, the saguaro is endangered—and some say, disappearing at an alarming rate. Pollution is its greatest enemy. Another is diminished habitat, as more and more of the desert is developed into real estate subdivisions, golf courses, and irrigated farming areas for truck crops. It is even the target of poachers, who dig up both old and young saguaros to sell to real estate developers. Guntoters looking for a formidable target shoot them full of holes just for the fun of it. Others become riddled with disease and insect attacks.

But there is reason to hope that a new page will be turned and somehow, we, the human population, will learn how to treat saguaros. More and more efforts are being made to protect them. Sometimes, even the saguaros fight back. A story in a Phoenix newspaper not so long ago told of a giant saguaro being used for target practice that actually fell upon one of the shooters, crushing him to death. Occasionally there is justice in the world, after all.

The abuse dealt to the great saguaros reminds me of a story from author-naturalist John Hay, who described seeing people on a New England beach torture a beached whale by sticking lighted cigarettes down its blowhole. The roadside vandals in Arizona are just as heartless, wielding not only firearms but clubs, rocks, and sharp knives to carve and whittle their own initials in the skin of these magnificent tree cacti.

Then there are the unknowns For instance, there's considerable mystery surrounding a period of some sixty years in the Saguaro National Monument where no reseeding and no renewal of growth took place in the saguaro forest. Nobody knows why. The natural reseeding has now been renewed, but no one knows why that happened, either.

128

Let's take a closer look at the Monument, which contains some 83,500 acres in two major tracts—the Rincon Tract on the east side of Tucson and the Tucson

Right. *Organ pipe cactus.*

Mountains unit west of the city. Both are literally covered with saguaros. It was these giant cacti that inspired President Herbert Hoover to preserve this region as "an outstanding scientific interest" in 1933, during the height of the Great Depression. At that time, the Rincon unit was by far the most impressive natural area, and scientists began studying it then. Very little at that time was known about cacti in general and the saguaro in particular. But then, for some mysterious reason, the saguaros began dying off. By 1991, the saguaro stand of Hoover's time had been reduced by more than 50 percent, and scientists now predict that the remaining mature saguaros in this unit will all be gone by the year 2000.

Scientists are baffled as to why this is happening. Some feel it may have been due to killer freezes, erratic summer rains, cattle grazing, wood cutting, air pollution, or the decline of the number of saguaro pollinators. Any one of these factors, they say, could have caused the problem. Or maybe a combination of them.

In the mid-1960s, botanist Raymond Turner and his colleagues of the U.S. Geological Survey in Tucson set up twenty saguaro monitoring plots throughout the 120,000-square-mile range, including both southwestern Arizona and the state of Sonora in old Mexico. In 1961 they counted 213 mature saguaros thriving in the Rincon plot east of Tucson. Thirty years later, only forty-two of those plants remained and many of those were in sad condition.

At the same time, however, researchers found 119 new plants, some only two to three feet in height, which had been seeded since 1960. Saguaros, of course, grow slowly, some only about five to six feet in half a century. But it is at least encouraging and somewhat comforting that the species is propagating itself. Despite this period of some sixty years when no reseeding took place, there will be replacements coming along. There will, however, be a long period of time—perhaps generations—when no old-growth saguaros will be alive in the Rincon unit.

Turner believes the real reason for the non-seeding was fluctuating rainfall amounts during that period of time and that this not only occurred in the Rincon Mountains, but also in the Pinacate Mountains of northern Sonora. Rainfall amounts can be critical during July and August, the natural germination period. From 1900 to 1960, rainfall amounts dropped far below their normal level of seven inches during this two-month period. Then, from 1960 to the present, summer rains have become more stable, and have either equalled or exceeded the seven-inch level.

Opposite, top. *Crested saguaro.*
Opposite, bottom. *The rib structure of the saguaro expands after heavy rains and contracts as the dry season progresses. The outer edges are protected by spiny thorns.*
Right. *The javelina is normally found in small family units of eight to ten.*

Cattle grazing may have been another harmful factor. In all of the affected areas, wood cutting and cattle grazing was permitted up until 1979. While cattle did not eat the saguaros, they did browse upon the paloverde and mesquite trees, which served as nurse plants to young saguaros, providing much-needed shelter from the blazing sun. Overgrazed areas also attracted ant colonies, another danger. Ants carry saguaro seeds underground, and even if the ants don't eat them, the seeds are left too deep in the earth to sprout.

Air pollution may also have been a continuing factor. The city of Tucson keeps spreading into the saguaro habitat, and the areas north and west of Phoenix are encroached upon as well by urban sprawl.

The valley where I first met the saguaros a quarter of a century ago, was, at that time, virtually without human inhabitants. Today, it is chock-full of houses. You don't realize it during the day, for the houses blend in well with the landscape. But at night the entire valley is lit up like a Christmas tree.

A fifty-year monitoring program has been set up by the National Park Service to test the effects of air pollution. Its goal is to determine whether such airborne pollutants as copper smelters, acid rain, auto emissions, herbicides, pesticides, or lime kilns (which once operated in this area) may have contributed or may yet be contributing to the demise of the saguaros.

While a good deal has been learned about all the cacti since the monument was established in the 1930s, there is much more yet to be learned. A desert specialist with the U.S. Geological Survey said we know very little. "Just look at this desert and tell me how any of these plants survive under everyday temperatures exceeding one hundred degrees with a rainfall that does not even reach a single foot in a whole year. But they do and we don't know how they do it."

But efforts are being made. In addition, and as a part of the monitoring station program, researchers in laboratories as far away as New Mexico, California, and New York are analyzing the composition of saguaro tissue and soil samples from the monument. In addition, young saguaros raised in laboratory situations are being exposed to varying levels of acid rain, just to see how they will react. Some feel the air pollution damages the saguaros' protective outer coating, the cuticle, which then speeds the spread of brown decline, reducing the plant's vigor and making it vulnerable to frost and other damage.

One researcher felt sure that the freeze was the Grim Reaper; air pollutants first lowered the tree's resistance, he says, predisposing them to that fate.

New growth may also be much affected by the lack of one of the tree's primary pollinators—the Sanborn long-nosed bat, which was placed on the endangered species list in 1988. These little bats feed nightly on agaves, organ pipes, and saguaros, on both the nectar and pollen. They depend upon caves, abandoned mines, and tunnels for roost sites. Researchers have determined that their demise is being brought about not only by the decline of nesting sites, but lack of food sources, and outright killing by humans. In Mexico, they are associated with blood-sucking vampire bats unpopular with the natives. They migrate far down into Central America during the fall, but return in the spring to the Sonoran Desert just in time to begin their great role as pollinator.

Although the loss of the bats doesn't necessarily mean the end of the saguaros,

All kinds of shapes and sizes of saguaros are found in the forest.

Bobcat kittens in the Sonoran Desert.

they do play a significant role. There are, however, other pollinators as well, such as cactus wrens, white-winged doves, and even honeybees.

Still another factor in the fight to save the saguaros is lightning. The Sonoran Desert has thousands of lightning strikes during the hot-weather months. Several years ago, 15,000 strikes were recorded in a single day in the Tucson area. Because of their great size, saguaros are in some ways like rods reaching upward to attract the lightning. Winds, too, bother them. Their roots do not penetrate deep into the shallow desert soil, but instead spread out on the surface, covering an area as much as eighty to a hundred feet in circumference. But once they get to rocking and reeling in high winds, they too often topple to the ground, sometimes because of their own immense weight.

Of course, many of these problems have plagued the saguaros for centuries. Lightning strikes and wind were likely just as much of a problem a thousand years ago. And long before the white man and air pollution arrived, there lived among the saguaro forest tribes of Indians.

The Papago and Pima tribes, the original human dwellers within the saguaro's domain, held the plant in higher esteem than we do today. In Papago legend, the saguaro was once human. In that long ago, they say, the saguaro was a little girl whose father was dead and whose mother often left her to fend for herself. In her neglect, the girl resigned her human condition, sank into the earth, and later reappeared as a strange plant none of the people had ever seen before. Taller and taller it grew, and when it had reached its full height, it bore a delicious fruit which has refreshed people to this day.

Perhaps the legend reflects the Papago's understanding that the young saguaro needs its nurse tree, just as all young things require nurture. Certainly life in the arid, lonesome stretches of their portion of the Sonoran Desert would have taught them this profound truth every day.

The Pima do not hold the grand old saguaros in such high position as do the Papago, but it does appear both in tribal lore and in practical ways. Pima legend ascribes the making of the first saguaro wine to the desert birds, several of whom soon got drunk on their new invention. According to the legend, the mockingbird was one of those who got drunk, and it began to talk incessantly, mocking all the other birds it knew. It continues, of course, to do so to this day.

In Indian culture, the saguaro became all-important. It was used to stimulate a mother's milk after childbirth, by feeding her a gruel made from the saguaro's fruit mixed with water and whole wheat. The fruit also was eaten as a dessert, and saguaro seeds, ground and roasted, were a substitute for lard. The Pima Indians also used the seeds as chicken feed and to tan leather, while the long wooden ribs were used as the framework for houses, splints, and basket frames.

The saguaro, while unquestionably the most impressive of the desert trees, is not alone. The paloverde seems to be gaining in numbers in the same forest where the saguaro grows, but it is not very large, nor does it age well. A fifty-year-old paloverde is a rarity. It is a tree virtually without foliage—the leaves are almost non-existent. It is a legume of the pea clan and seldom reaches a height of more than twenty feet tall. I'm sure it plays a good many important roles in the desert ecology, but its most impressive role is to provide shade as a nurse plant for the young saguaros desperately trying to survive. If a baby saguaro does not have a nurse, it may perish simply from the harsh desert sun.

I became aware as I spent time in the desert that life and death are closer to each other there than anyplace I'd ever been before. Few things can hide in this merciless landscape, and only the hardiest survive. Perhaps this is part of the desert's fascination.

There is both great similarity and great diversity in deserts. In the southwestern portions of the Sonoran Desert the cacti tree cover varies from the giant saguaro to the organ pipe and, in Mexico, the senita, which much resembles the organ pipe but is taller, growing up to thirty feet. The organ pipe seldom reaches upward more than twenty feet. While the organ pipe and senita also are tree cacti with wooden skeletons, they do not resemble a tree nearly as much in any other way. They both grow in clusters, with single shafts and no protruding arms. They grow only on south-facing slopes, so if you drive to such places as Organ Pipe National Monument on the Mexican-Arizona border, you will see few organ pipe cacti unless you look in your rear-view mirror. That's because you're driving south and they'll be behind you. In the United States, the Monument is about the only place you'll see organ pipe cacti, but they grow rampant in Sonora. The Monument was set aside by presidential proclamation in 1937 mostly to call attention to this unique landscape.

The Sonoran is a prolific desert. Perhaps no other desert in the world has a greater variety of plant life or enjoys such lush growth. During half of the year it is exceedingly green; and some springs it is a veritable flower garden. A variety of cacti and other plants adorn the *bajada* or rocky slope of this desert: teddybears; varieties of the cholla cactus such as the chain, jumping, pencil, and hedgehog; prickly pear, mesquite, and ocotillo. In April, after exceedingly heavy winter rains, the desert world becomes a dazzling landscape. Every plant, it seems, tries to outdo its neighbor in its display of bright colors.

At this time, too, everything else in the desert becomes very active. The nights are filled with the sounds of wailing coyotes. Wolf spiders emerge to prey upon other insects; hairy tarantulas are everywhere. All kinds of songbirds dart about the desert, and tiny elf owls peer from their dens in old saguaros. Packs of coatimundi prowl the desert landscape. Bobcats, cougars, ocelots, chuckwallas, and Gila monsters, a dozen different kinds of snakes including tiger and blacktail rattlers, and the comic roadrunners all may be seen at any time. The desert in the spring is a most fascinating place.

West and north of the Sonoran Desert lies the Mojave, mostly in California. It's a different kind of desert, with volcanic boulders spewed across the landscape, very sparse vegetation, and in some parts, small forests of Joshua trees. Botanists are quick to point out this is not a tree at all, but an agave plant that thinks it's a tree. It has no growth rings and therefore no age notes by which man can tell just how old a Joshua tree is. Most scientists believe that the older ones live to be no more than 150 years old. But they don't know for sure. There is no monitoring process.

The Joshua tree for all the world looks like a tree, and that, of course, is the reason they are called trees. In different places it has been called a tree yucca, desert plant, giant yucca, or praying plant. But it became a tree in earnest when the early pioneers happened upon it when wagon trains first rolled into California from the east. Because of its many upstretched branches, or arms, which they thought resembled Joshua waving them onward, they christened it the Joshua tree. And while botanists and foresters, insist that it's not a true tree, this is still its most commonly accepted name.

One of the oldest known desert plants, the Joshua tree is limited to a few small isolated areas. Scientists believe it may have been widespread in the Southwest during more humid prehistoric times, but today its domain is the Mojave uplands, where it grows mostly above 3000 feet. It apparently needs cold winters for an essential dormant period. At these elevations in the Mojave, annual precipitation averages only eight to ten inches, with some of it coming in summer showers at a time when germination is taking place.

The Joshua tree is fickle. If you change any of the above ingredients, the tree likely will not survive. Only a few small segments of Nevada, Utah, California, and Arizona meet its criteria for existence. The greatest Joshua tree forests are found within the boundaries of the Joshua Tree National Monument in southern California, some two hours east of Los Angeles. Here specimens rise to forty feet in height and up to four feet in diameter at the base. And there are lots of them.

Like any woodland, the Joshua forest is a composite of unbranched infants, Medusa-crowned elders, old patriarchs, and everything in between.

Be it tree or non-tree, the Joshua tree is a remarkable member of the desert landscape. The fact that it exists at all is of some wonderment. It relies upon a small insect known as the Navajo yucca borer, or yucca moth, for pollination. The deliberate fertilization occurs sporadically. Only pollinated flowers produce the seeds required to feed the moth larvae, which hatch from eggs carefully deposited in the flower ovary. After the moths are hatched they devour both plant fibers and seeds, but enough are left over for the wind to shake free and scatter across the desert floor. Only when the temperature and rainfall are somehow ecologically balanced do

Joshua tree forest, Mojave Desert, California.

Above. *The mountain lion is found in the more mountainous and rocky areas of the Sonoran Desert.*
Left. *The woody understructure of the great saguaro.*
Opposite. *Beaver (shown here), otter, and even waterfowl are found at desert oases.*

138

the yucca moths hatch. And only in wetter years do the huge, pineapple-shaped flowers blossom. So a good many years may pass without a single Joshua tree blossom.

The tree begins its life as a single spike with a single dense cluster of needle-tipped leaves at its crown. It develops branches only after the yucca moth has eaten into the tree buds, causing it to send out another arm bypassing the damaged portion. So because of sporadic flowering activity allowing the yucca moth activity, it may take a tree many years to accumulate the double- and triple-joined limbs which distinguish it as an elder. Tests at the Joshua Tree National Monument show the annual growth rate to be about three inches per year for the first ten years and only about half that in subsequent years.

In some areas of the Mojave, where temperatures are consistently too cold during winter or where the soil is extremely rocky or acid, stunted Joshua tree forests exist with 150-year-old trees no taller than one's head. And in these areas, they never blossom during their entire lifespan.

The Joshua tree plays a vital role in many other ways, however. At least twenty-five species of birds are known to use it for nest sites. When a tree dies, insect larvae, termites, spiders, beetles, and ants all are drawn to it for food and shelter. The yucca night lizard prefers it to all other places to live. Deer, squirrels, and birds feast on the sweet blossoms and fleshy fruits. Antelope ground squirrels stockpile the seeds for winter. A host of desert creatures would suffer were there not a Joshua tree.

As one looks at the total desert perspective, it soon becomes apparent that the Joshua tree fills an important niche. It survives in a geographical and geological locale where nothing else can, foresting what otherwise would be an unforgiving landscape. But the desert is like that; life is at a premium here, but there is always something to fill the niches.

EIGHT

Methuselah Trees

I n the western alpine slopes of the high Sierras live the emperors of the tree kingdom. The giant sequoias, found in some seventy groves between 4500 and 8000 feet in altitude are the oldest and mightiest of living things on earth. Because of their immense size and unbelievable age, every one of them deserves to be declared an official monument, sacred among nature's finest creations. They are the largest trees on the entire planet. Nothing else comes close.

What's more, these huge trees are nearly immortal, having stood for thousands upon thousands of years. Nothing seems to affect them except man, and one hopes human greed has now been channeled in another direction. None of the great sequoias have ever met their demise from disease, insects, animals, or other adverse natural elements, or even old age. They continue to grow as long as they live, and each one standing is very much alive.

Some 250 miles to the west, the second-largest trees on the planet—the fog-breathing-redwoods—occupy the secluded coves of the Pacific coast. They are taller, but lack the girth of their mountaineering cousins. Their age is something less than thirty centuries; the sequoias may indeed be double that or even more, so old they almost defy our concept of what time is about.

Introduced to the California Big Trees, as they are sometimes called, at Sequoia National Park, I found them more spellbinding than any natural attraction I had ever seen. Niagara Falls, the Grand Canyon, Old Faithful—none of these even came close to the awe I now felt as I stood at the base of the General Sherman, straining my neck to look upward. The Four Guardsmen near the entrance who had ushered me into the park didn't look old, just huge. So huge one automatically knew they were aged beyond belief. I had come to associate old age with deformity; trees I had known

Opposite. *Even in groves, sequoias tend to claim space around them, giving room for younger trees to grow.*

before, like the bristlecone pines along the California-Nevada border, the giant mesquite in the Mojave Desert, even the 400-year-old live oaks draped with whiskers of gray Spanish moss in my own Florida woods—all were twisted and turned by so many years' exposure to the elements. But these monoliths grew straight and tall as the heavens to which they pointed.

I had been working on a field photography project on California's Channel Islands when I wrested a few days' reprieve to drive to Sequoia and Kings Canyon national parks. What a reprieve it was to be. No one would ever believe the size of these trees back home. To provide some measure of comparison, I parked my Chinook mini-motorhome in a grove and, with a wide-angle lens, captured some images on film. Even as I looked through the camera's viewfinder, I could hardly believe my eyes. The Methuselah trees were so large, some measuring 100 feet in circumference, and so tall, that some—were they in a city—would throw shadows atop a twelve-story building.

I was told that the General Grant tree is 271 feet high; the Boole tree, at sixteen feet above the ground, is still twenty-five feet in diameter; and the Hart tree is the tallest of all sequoias at 281 feet, six inches. There's even a strong possibility that an even taller tree which has not been measured lives among the groves of the Sierra Nevada.

Upon the ground in the Calaveras North Grove lies the tree sometimes referred to as the Father of the Forest, inside whose hollow trunk a man can ride horseback without having to bend his head; it's been done. The bark on some of these giants is two feet thick, almost like armament, one reason almost nothing gets to the heart of these trees. Even serious forest fires rarely burn through the bark; a case has been recorded of a lightning strike in the top of a giant sequoia setting off a blaze that burned for thirty days without serious damage to the tree.

The Wawona Tree in Mariposa Cove was tunneled in 1881, and for years was a favorite in the park because folks could drive their automobiles through it. It fell from a windthrow in 1969 before I had a chance to enjoy that experience, but there are a couple of trees among the redwoods along the fog-shrouded coast of California where you can still do that. One of them is the Chandelier Tree at Leggett, which towers 315 feet above a twenty-one-foot diameter base.

So hardy and bent upon living are these trees that one, the Sawed Tree in Kings Canyon National Park, was cut almost entirely through by loggers nearly a century ago but refused to fall. Lumberjacks finally abandoned it, and today new growth has virtually covered the scar, and given the tree new strength. Another, the Tennessee Tree, was nearly destroyed by fire near its base. Little more than an outer shell supported it, but one scar more than a foot wide and nine feet high has been completely filled in with new growth. One named the Stricken Tree still thrives, although lightning in the early part of this century shattered the upper portions, hurling hundreds of large pieces seventy-five feet or more.

Many of the trees within Sequoia and Kings Canyon national parks have been named individually over the years, but the species became known as sequoia after the half-breed Cherokee Indian genius Sequoyah, who devised the Cherokee alphabet during the early nineteenth century. It is claimed that the German botanist Stephen Endlicher, who was among those doing studies on the big trees, named

Sequoia National Park.

them in the Cherokee's honor. The spelling of the name was then changed to sequoia. In 1890, Congress designated Sequoia National Park, the first one in California.

The sequoias grow mostly in scattered coves, and they seem to be a community tree; they are rarely found alone or isolated from others of their species. The territory they now occupy, although remnants of ancient logs dating back more than 10,000 years have been discovered by scientists all the way from northern British Columbia into the Rockies of the United States, ranges along a 260-mile stretch of the western slopes of the Sierras. It includes some 35,600 acres. Scientifically, they are referred to as *Sequoiadendron giganteum* while the coastal redwoods are *Sequoia sempervirens.* The latter occupy some two million acres along the northern California coast from Big Sur, south of San Francisco, into southern Oregon.

Significant similarities exist between the two trees, but there also are some notable differences as well. To begin, the bark color is different: redwoods, dark brown with a grayish tint; sequoias, rich reddish brown. The bark of the redwoods is only about a foot thick; sequoias, two feet thick. The cones of the redwood are about an inch long (very small for such a huge tree), while sequoia cones are about three inches long. Needles of sequoias are small and scalelike while those of the redwoods are needlelike. There are other differences too, like the way they grow and the weight density of the wood, but many of these distinctions are merely academic. The most

143

Some of these giant trees are more than four thousand years old.

Sequoia National Park.

noteworthy one to me is the height—redwoods are substantially taller than the sequoias. This may be due in part to the amounts of rainfall—100 inches a year for the coastal redwoods; 45 to 60 inches for the sequoias. The sequoias may be substantially older, too, since coastal redwoods seldom have been found to exceed 2500 years of age.

A third member of the sequoia family was discovered near the end of World War II, growing in a remote mountainous region of China. Known as the dawn redwood *(Metasequoia),* it also once grew in California, as well as considerable other parts of the planet. It resembles the coastal redwoods in some respects, but it is a deciduous conifer.

Naturalist John Muir, who is perhaps best known as the founder of the Sierra Club, spent years hiking the high Sierras in search of still more groves of sequoias. Among his findings were logs of *S. gigantea,* some more than 10,000 years old, straddled by other living sequoias of great age. Muir concluded after his fruitless search that the sequoias already had established their habitat long before European man came to this continent. Friend to several U.S. presidents and congressmen as well as governors of California, Muir was, however, unsuccessful in his long campaign to have all the territory occupied by the giant trees set aside for posterity. A portion of it became national park, but there is still, to this day, a vast area within the boundaries of the Sequoia National Forest that is largely unprotected. As late as the mid-1980s, many trees were harvested, until environmentalists discovered the cutting and brought court action to put a stop to it.

Although Muir is credited, and rightly so, for his concern and exploration of the big trees, it was some years before him that one A.T. Dowd, while chasing bear one day in 1852, came suddenly upon them. He was so astonished and overwhelmed he let the bear get away, but he hurried back to camp to tell others of his find. Many fellow miners came hurriedly to look, for they could not believe Dowd's story. What they found was apparently the Calaveras North Grove, with giants reaching upward some 325 feet and more than twenty feet in diameter. They simply called them the "Mammoth Trees." A month later someone had already passed along some of the seeds to a California botanist, Dr. Albert Kellogg, who did absolutely nothing with them. Two years later, however, he showed specimens of branches, leaves, and cones to one William Lobb, who immediately set out to collect more. Lobb recently had arrived in California to collect plants for a British nursery, but what Kellogg told him was bigger news. Once Lobb had visited and collected more from the groves, he hurried to San Francisco and took the first boat to London. There he turned his collection over to the British botanist John Lindley, who in 1854 published an article on the trees. He named them *Wellingtonia gigantea,* in honor of the Duke of Wellington.

American botanists were furious, but they had no right to be; after all, Kellogg had known about the trees a full two years before the British. It was only because another article published in Germany six years previously had named the big trees *Sequoia* that the name was maintained.

About this same time a disappointed gold seeker, G.H. Woodruff of the state of New York, climbed up into the sequoia groves to rest. Examining some cones tossed down by chickarees, he shook out the seeds, put them in an empty snuff box, and shipped it to a nursery firm in Rochester, New York. From these tiny seeds sprang nearly 4000 little trees. They didn't sell well in New York, but they did in England, where they still were known as *Wellingtonias.* Botanical gardens all over England, France, and Germany wanted specimens. Later, they spread to the Pyrenees of France and Spain. As a result of this widespread sequoia fad, large trees thrive in many parts of England and Spain to this day. They do not experience the fast growth of California, probably because of varied climatic conditions, but they do thrive.

No one really knows why the sequoias live so long. One theory claims that it's the great amounts of tannic acid in the tree, the acid prevents senility and keeps it growing until it is either weakened by lightning and subsequent fire in the crown, or windtoppled when its root system, which at its peak period of growth may cover as much as an acre of ground, becomes weakened. Absolutely nothing on earth save the heartbeat of a turtle defies death so fiercely. I've seen a turtle's heart beat for days even after removed from the body. And the sequoia's lust for life is similar; once fallen, it may take ten years or more for the foliage to wither.

All this eternal life comes from a flaky seed so small it takes 3000 of them to weigh an ounce. The seed kernel is just a quarter-inch long and inside it lies the embryonic monarch, curled and waiting for just the right moment to be hurled to the ground below. About 300 seeds are produced in a single tight cone. To release the seeds, nature employs the help of hundreds of jaybirds and a most active little chickaree, a member of the squirrel family that eats the fleshy scales of sequoia cones and does not bother with the tiny seeds. Sequoias produce few seeds until the second century of their life, but then, on good sites, they may bear as many as 40,000 cones. A single chickaree may harvest as many as 10,000 cones in a solitary season. Multiply that number by 300 seeds per cone and you have three million seeds tossed to the winds.

The tiny cones of a giant sequoia.

A nurse log, perhaps centuries on the ground, provides a soft bed for all kinds of new growth, mosses, lichens, and even little trees.

Inside a sequoia, the wood is soft and brittle.

Mayapples, which bear a yellowish, soft, edible fruit, grow among the redwood groves.

Redwoods National Park.

Because the seeds bed themselves much easier if the forest floor is relatively clean, foresters and naturalists agree that fire also plays a very positive role in preparing a welcome seedbed. If the seed lands on forest duff—decaying leaves and branches—instead of bare mineral soil, it most likely will never germinate and take root. Foresters claim the chances of a single seed becoming a giant sequoia is about a billion to one. The odds are about the same for the coastal redwood.

The redwoods, of course, have been much more threatened by man's logging operations than have the sequoias. The wood of the sequoia is brittle. Early logging operations there were very difficult with such huge trees. In some cases it took four men nearly a month just to cut down a single sequoia. Then it was discovered in most cases that the tree, when it came crashing down, would break into a hundred pieces, and the logs were often not worth hauling off to the sawmill. Special equipment had to be designed to haul the intact logs. This was not the case with the coastal redwoods, which were quite pliable and not brittle at all.

Consequently, whole groves of sequoias were cut but the logs never marketed. You can see them in Sequoia and Kings Canyon national parks to this day. Smaller,

148

The parking area at the Lady Bird Johnson Cove of redwoods in California.

less mature trees were harvested, however, and could be again if environmentalists do not keep a keen watch on what's happening in the woods.

Since the big trees were discovered, mankind has felt compelled to do strange things with them. No one really knows why, but early on folks tunneled through the base of at least one of them, so they could drive first with horses and carriages and later with automobiles through the tree. If it were still standing today, some daring drivers would doubtless be challenged to drive two small cars through side-by-side at the same time. A huge tree that blew down in 1917 was dubbed Auto Log. It fell perpendicular to the road and the park superintendent promptly had a trestle built so horse-drawn carriages and automobiles could be driven onto the log. It's about 245 feet long, and it may come as some surprise that a raceway hasn't been built atop it for dragsters or sprint cars. The trestle has now been replaced by a paved ramp. Many a car has been photographed looking very tiny atop the huge log.

Both the sequoias and coastal redwoods belong to the age of the dinosaurs—and they have only narrowly avoided the dinosaurs' fate. Were it not for a few staunch men and women who took up the fight to save them, doubtless all would long ago

149

Above. *Depending upon the density of the canopy, some redwood groves allow a fair amount of understory to thrive.* Left. *Remnants from the life of a great sequoia.*

have been destroyed and turned into building materials, railroad crossties, or fence posts.

One of the most noted preservation efforts was made by the Save-the-Redwoods League, formed in 1918. For half a century, it struggled to get some areas set aside along the coastal range which extends from southwest Oregon to Big Sur—a strip averaging only twenty to thirty miles wide. With matching funds provided by the state of California, the League was finally able to place some redwood forests in the California State Park System. These include Prairie Creek Redwoods, Jedediah Smith, and Del Norte Coast Redwoods.

The League fought a tough battle during the 1920s and '30s to get such a park established. Studies were made and in 1946, just a year after World War II ended, it appeared that the Douglas Bill, proposing a memorial national forest of 2.5 million acres with about 180,000 acres to be preserved, would be approved by Congress. It didn't because the timber companies pumped so much money into the fight against it.

Nearly twenty years later, the National Park Service conducted a survey of the region. Their findings showed some critical situations. Of the original growth forest of nearly two million acres, only 15 percent remained, and of that amount, only 2.5 percent or approximately 50,000 acres was protected. Redwoods which were old when Columbus discovered America were almost no more. If cutting were allowed to continue at its 1960s pace, virtually all of the remaining redwoods would be cut by the turn of the century. The legendary trees would be just that—legend, things to be talked about in the past tense.

The first successful effort on behalf of the coastal redwoods came in 1902 with the establishment of Big Basin Redwoods State Park near Santa Cruz. Then came Muir Woods just north of San Francisco, set aside as a gift from Congressman William Kent to the federal government in honor of the great naturalist. The last time I was in Muir Woods, it was a sunny Sunday afternoon. People were everywhere, walking the trails, picnicking, having fun. I was alone, and I thought about those great trees that perhaps had known Muir personally. He had probably walked there as I now walked there, but without the crowds. We had a great deal in common, I thought, for I, too, had spent much of my life attempting to educate people about the true values of their natural environment and, in my own quiet way, campaigning for the rights of trees, wild animals, birds, and all life forms with which we share the planet.

The sunny day was out of character for the coastal redwoods forest. These great trees survive—no, thrive—on foggy days. The shade that fog provides is vital to redwoods, as is the extra ration of water condensing from mist to drops and percolating from leaf to limb to ground. During long summer days of direct sunlight the fog is a protective parasol against transpiration and evaporation. Due to its own limiting factors of temperature and vaporizing, the fog thins out south of the Santa Cruz Mountains, its northerly tide spent. In response to their own limitations, the redwoods become sparse and then disappear; without fog there can be no redwoods. That is the chief reason they are found in such a narrow band along the Pacific Coast.

The coastal redwoods are sensitive to cold, salt water, and high winds. They like gentle rains, cool breezes, long summers, and no snow. On the other hand, sequoias thrive on snow which normally piles ten to fifteen feet deep in the high Sierras every winter. They do not respond well to temperatures below zero, but otherwise they thrive fairly well with far fewer requirements than the coastal redwoods.

While the coastal redwood does not produce the large amounts of seeds of the sequoia, or even other conifers such as the Douglas fir, it does sprout new saplings from the roots, logs, and stumps of long-gone trees. This may explain the rings of redwoods, some of them old-growth, seen standing here and there about the forest. They are trees which have been born around the perimeter of an old stump centuries ago.

In one area of the park, scientists have found evidence of extensive destruction, most likely from a volcano. Some five million years ago, trees were thrown down and tossed aside like matchsticks, much like the forests were destroyed by the eruption of Mt. St. Helens in Washington a few years ago. All the tops pointed to the south, and the trees were buried beneath volcanic ash. The greatest of the fallen trees were redwoods, but with them were found spruces, hemlocks, Douglas fir, red alder, tanoak, chinquapin, huckleberry, rhododendron, and wax myrtle. Trees and shrubs not familiar to the area since—water chestnut, normally found only in China; red bay, elm, and chestnut, all trees of the eastern United States—were also found.

Today, the coastal redwoods and their cousins, the Sierra sequoias, are living symbols of continuity. They span eons of time, and bridge the ages of yesterday and today. They represent something far greater and more timeless than humankind. We must realize that the great trees were not created for our use and abuse. We are often Lilliputian both in our size and our thinking when it comes to the Methuselah trees.

Left. *This massive sequoia log may have been lying here for more than a thousand years.*

Log jams form in swales which collect other debris to form veritable mulch beds in the forest.

NINE

The Pygmy Forest

A long the restless Pacific Ocean from southern California well into Canada's British Columbia time has created a terraced staircase. Although obscured by vegetation and so large at more than 300 yards that the human eye tends to overlook them, the steps are truly there, a rare study in geological history. Created by the process of rising and falling tides as well as varying ocean levels dictated by freezing and thawing glaciers over millenium, this staircase through time might well have gone unnoticed.

On some of these terraces live some of the world's largest trees, the California redwoods. On others, alongside and adjacent, lives a pygmy forest with ancient trees no taller than an average man. These two forests are similar in age, but the pygmy forest is one of the most phenomenal forests found on earth.

Old growth forest is often considered the ultimate development of tree growth, but the trees covering this staircase are among the most distinctive trees found anywhere. Although they are found all up and down the United States and Canada coastline, perhaps nowhere else can they be better observed than in the Jug Handle Creek watershed in California's Mendocino County north of San Francisco. In this outdoor museum one can observe the genesis of a shoreline and unravel the mystery of the pygmy forest and the five giant steps that have been created and lifted above the sea.

Geologists figure that the five broad, wave-cut terraces, some dissected with volcanic or earthquake canyons and further enhanced by erosion from the heavy ocean-borne wind and rains, were formed during the past half-million years. Each step is about one hundred feet higher and 100,000 years older than the one immediately below it. On the steps closer to the sea live the giant redwood, cypress, and Douglas fir.

Opposite. *None of these trees are more than six to eight feet tall, yet they are 350-400 years old.*

Armed with this information and a battery of heavy cameras, some of my family and I some years ago first invaded the step country in search of the evasive pygmy forest. It would be difficult to find, I figured. Not like looking for giant redwoods. These trees, I had been told, were not only diminutive, but in many instances, they would not appear as trees at all, but instead shrubs. One might stumble right through shrub and be in Douglas fir again before one knew it.

My middle and youngest sons, Billy and Alan, accompanied me and when we alighted from our motorhome, I gathered them for a briefing. "These trees might remind you of bonsai," I cautioned. "They may be no taller than you are, but they could be and probably are ancient."

"What's a bonsai?" asked Alan. He had seen them at a bonsai garden near the nation's capitol only a year or two before, but had apparently forgotten all about that. And I could see by the look on fourteen-year-old Billy's face that he thought I was pulling his leg. But once briefed, they gathered up an array of camera gear, film, and some lunch items—for we didn't know just how long we might be in pursuit of the pygmy forest—and we set off.

Luck was with us. In less than half an hour we came upon small, stunted trees, and in no time at all we found ourselves in the midst of a true forest of warped and twisted trees. Pygmy cypress, Bolander pine, dwarf bishop pine, and a large array of shrubs and herbaceous plants of the heath family surrounded us, an otherworldly setting.

I stopped and surveyed this strange forest in every direction. The boys were silent; it wasn't as though we were now deep in a cathedral forest and yet, because of the age of these little trees, we knew we stood upon sacred ground. This forest was unique; the more you looked, the more you saw. The majority of trees were no more than knee high. Yet they obviously were fully mature trees with cones and catkins hanging from their limbs.

The trunks of these ancients were gnarled and twisted, their bark split and weathered by the elements and half-hidden beneath lichens of many shapes and colors. Their branches were musty and grotesque with hanging moss. They were old, worn, and mysterious. They seemed as if they had once reached to the heavens but, by some strange force, had been suddenly reduced to Lilliputian dimensions.

The growth here appeared brittle and ill-formed and most fragile. We were careful in touching anything. It was almost like touching rare and valuable antiques. I half expected a booming voice from somewhere deep in the forest directing us to leave and never come back.

The ground was hard and lacked humus, just the opposite of what I had found in almost all the old-growth forests I had visited. "What in the world had happened here?" I thought. I had been told by the California Department of Geology that this was indeed a climax forest. These trees were indeed 300 to 400 years old, yet in diameter they measured less than six inches at the base.

Alan who was only four feet tall himself, singled out a Bolander pine that soared a good eight feet above him.

"Look, Dad, here's a big one," he shouted, adjusting his old Cincinnati Reds baseball cap that was several sizes too large to keep the sun out of his eyes. I worried he'd get a crick in his neck looking upward. "Watch it doesn't fall on you," I warned.

Foot trails lead through the pygmy forest, allowing one to actually look down upon some 300-year-old trees.

Sitting down upon the hard ground (there wasn't a single tree here strong enough to lean against), I pondered this unusual forest as my sons gathered around.

"Sort of baffles the imagination, doesn't it?"

They agreed. It was a tough photographic challenge. How does one show diminutive trees in a true nature setting where there were no normal-sized trees to compare them to? One could photograph the twisted, gnarled appearance of singular trees. I decided to try for that plus an overview. And that might not be impressive, either. It turned out I was right.

For a few hours we fiddled around in the strangest forest I had ever encountered. The boys were getting restless and I was getting perplexed. What to do, and how to do it? I decided there was little more I could accomplish. Certainly almost nothing lived here; a lizard had scampered across the path to hide among the hoary bark on a dwarf bishop pine. A butterfly flitted through and somewhere I heard a bird call I could not identify. But it was from beyond the pygmy forest.

Fungus gall infections are common in the pygmy forest trees, suggestive of specific nutrient deficiencies.

It was plain to see nothing much ever happened here, and what did occurred over thousands of years. Had one been able to witness it firsthand, one probably would still be unaware of its progress. I thought about that for a moment, gazing from one tree to another. There. Over there was a specimen that probably hadn't changed a bit since Christopher Columbus wandered across the Atlantic. Four hundred years! It looked more dead than alive. But it was alive, and if it could recount history in someway I could understand, what fun it would be to listen. It had barely occurred to me when Alan spoke, wondering the same thing. Strange how such ideas come to us when we see something really old that transcends a human lifespan. It happens more in the ancient forest, I speculated, than in any other environment on earth. Because nothing else so alive is quite so old.

Here the changes between the very small and the very large occur rather dramatically, sometimes within just a few feet. Just over there the redwoods and Douglas fir were huge. A few feet away, unforgettable primal pygmy forest.

158

In British Columbia, there are excellent examples, some even more expansive than the Jug Handle Creek one. Others exist in other parts of California and along the

Overview of the pygmy forest at Jug Handle State Preserve, California.

Pacific Coast. But at no place is the staircase formation more complete nor accessible than here. It is believed to be the only place where each step of shoreline development can be seen virtually intact.

During the Pleistocene Age, one to two million years ago, glaciers expanded and receded numerous times. When they froze up and extended their tongues southward to create another Ice Age on the land, the oceans, of course, supplied the water and thus dropped in sea level. When the sea was fairly stable, the wave action created terraces along the shorelines. In the dark-gray sandstones (called graywackes) of Mendocino County, a platform several hundred feet wide was formed. Geologic forces, sometimes volcanic or caused by earthquakes, elevated the terraces. Today five distinct ones can be identified here, at elevations of 100, 200, 300, 425, and 650 feet. A new terrace is presently being carved by the sea, and at low tide it is distinctly visible. From the ocean to the edge of the oldest terrace is about three miles.

The dwarfed vegetation of the old-growth pygmy forest is the result of both the chemical composition and the physical composition of the beach soil. In this case, the beach materials underwent intense chemical leaching. Some minerals weathered to form clay, and some of their base components were carried off by waters percolating through the soil. Soon, the percolating waters mobilized soluble minerals, and during dry spells they hardened into a crusted, impenetrable pan. The recrystalization of the minerals created a huge pan so tough no roots penetrated it. It took 300,000 years to reach that point.

Plants that chose to live here had to learn to do so without roots reaching the depth that would sustain growth. Instead, they survived but grew ever so slowly—for lack of water, lack of minerals, and lack of humus. Eventually, the soil developed a bleached, gray color. The fertility level fell so low that nutrient-demanding redwoods and Douglas firs could not survive. They tried and they died.

Consequently, the pygmy forest only covers about 74 percent of the land, with the remaining 26 percent bare or covered with colonies of lichens. Dwarfed shrubs on the 74 percent include Labrador tea, rose bay, two species of manzanita, huckleberry, and salal. Gall infections, die-back symptoms, and fungus are rampant. Clearly, life here is most difficult.

The California Department of Parks and Recreation had the foresight to set aside for posterity a thousand acres of the area around Jug Handle Creek. It was a commendable act, for it is truly an extraordinary place. When we first entered the area, it did not seem inviting; by the time we were ready to leave, we did so with reluctance.

As we left the forest, I said to my sons, "You probably have never been, or ever will be, at another place on this planet where you can truly experience what a pygmy forest was like half a million years ago. "Here all you have to do is walk three miles west, 500 feet down and half a million years into the past. And you can do it in half a day."

I was happy that had struck a chord in their young minds and provoked them to thought. I knew it would come back to them many times in years to come, and they would remember these few hours in this unique landscape.

Pygmy forests are not unique to the Pacific coast. They are found in small plots at various locales in other parts of America. The Pine Barrens of New Jersey possess a few hundred acres; there are others in the permafrost soils of Alaska where ice layers restrict root penetration. In Florida, too, there are stands of dwarf forests. A stand of dwarf cypress can be reached from the main road leading to Flamingo station in the Everglades National Park.

But the three terraces of stunted old-growth forest in Mendocino County are unique. They represent the true genesis of a plant community reaching geologically back into the Pleistocene. It transcends the ages in a special kind of way. In 1969, the U.S. Department of the Interior recognized the uniqueness of this place, declaring it a National Natural Landmark.

Well, I've been back to visit the pygmy forest upon several occasions since that first introduction. My sons have all grown up now and moved away to seek their own forests. Each time I visit Jug Handle Creek, I am reminded of that first visit and Alan's "big tree"; it has not grown that I can see, or changed in any way. As if in defiance of time itself, it lives on unchanged through the years in its stable environment while the larger world out there goes spinning past.

Opposite. *An army of dwarf trees.*

TEN

Woods of the Deep South

The sweet, heavy scent of blossoming magnolia permeated the air as I hiked a balmy woodland trail leading to Bee Branch in the Sipsey Wilderness Area of northern Alabama. Only recently, Congress had officially designated this 12,726-acre forest as wilderness to be preserved for posterity. I was both glad and anxious to explore what I had been told was one of the most interesting forests in the entire South. It was a cool day in April 1975; the trees still bore that vibrant new green that comes with the spring equinox.

Old leaves and needles crunched underfoot as I made my way for more than a mile on a little-used trail through the woods. There was no old growth here, but that would soon change as I reached the canyon that contained Bee Branch. The whole area was being administered by the U.S. Forest Service as part of the Bankhead National Forest. At the time, it represented the first wilderness area in the entire eastern United States.

Dogwood just past spring blossom, sugar maple, sweet gum, hickory, and umbrella magnolia adorned the forest. When the trail came suddenly to the rim of a rock canyon precipice that dropped some seventy feet almost straight down, some of the vegetation changed. The density of the canopy overhead increased; only shafts of sunlight here and there penetrated to reach the forest floor. The trail disappeared into the walls of the canyon; from this point easy hiking suddenly turned into a cautious pick-your-step, foot-by-foot crawl as it switchbacked precariously downward. In most places, there wasn't even room to place your foot down flat. I scanned the rock ledges above and below me for copperheads and rattlesnakes that might claim this as their own private sunbathing area. Slowly and carefully I picked my way down to the floor of the canyon, which leveled off for several hundred yards. All about me giant

163

Opposite. *This tree spreads its roots over a rock, rather than entering its crevices, in the Sipsey Wilderness, Alabama.*

Spiderwort.

Centipede, Sipsey Wilderness.

trees, among them great eastern hemlock, towered to the sky. A slight wind stirred the canopy, which stretched far beyond the rim of the canyon. All around me I could hear the sounds of running water, although it had not rained for several days. The rocks of the canyon walls were fairly dripping with it, and the vines and clumps of weedy vegetation glistened in the light. I walked slowly on, drinking in this verdant, refreshing woodland. Ferns and wildflowers—wild geraniums, daisylike coreopsis, wood betony, and sweet cicely—grew profusely in groups here and there.

Suddenly, as I walked toward the sound of rushing water, I came upon the most stately tree in this forest. Simply called Big Tree, a state-record tulip poplar with a girth of more than twenty feet, it towered more than 150 feet toward a darkening Alabama sky. It was obvious a spring storm was brewing; my visit to Bee Branch might be cut short.

For a good thirty minutes, I examined and admired Big Tree. Then I continued making my way toward running water. I could soon see it—two thin, fifty-foot waterfalls cascading over the canyon rim behind Big Tree, feeding crystal pools at their base. I wanted to take off my shoes and go wading in the cold waters, but such thoughts were brought to an end by the roll of heavy thunder in the distance. Packing up my camera gear, I clambered up the steep trail and raced through the scant woods to my parking place. The mile I had hiked into the forested canyon seemed like three coming back, and my breath came in quick gasps. By the time I reached safety, lightning was bouncing off the ground around me and drops of rain began to plummet from the turbulent clouds above me. The storm broke full force as I escaped in my car.

Since I had only been able to get away for a few hours (I had driven down from Muscle Shoals on the Tennessee River, where I was doing a fishing story for *Sports Afield*) this fleeting experience of the Sipsey would not be repeated in the near future.

Opposite. *Sipsey Wilderness.*

Right. *A woodland wedding in Alabama old growth.*
Below. *A stream's quiet solitude in the Sipsey.*

But I vowed to return with more time to explore and enjoy the big trees of this old-growth forest wilderness—sometime when it wasn't stormy.

It would be six years before destiny again led me to Bee Branch. This time it was while on assignment for *National Geographic.* Upon checking in at the Forest Service headquarters, I learned that an unusual wedding was being planned for Bee Branch. It was to be held under Big Tree only two days later and I decided to make a point of being there. I didn't want to be a part of the wedding ceremony, but it sounded so unusual, I decided it would be interesting to watch. Besides, I didn't have a tuxedo, and all members of the wedding party would be dressed formally—black tie and tux for the men, evening gowns for the women.

Moreover, I was told the bride would be married barefoot and that the couple would make their escape after the wedding in a canoe—floating down Bee Branch, which was barely wide enough to squeeze a canoe around the turns down to Sipsey Fork and beyond. Fascinating, I thought. It was springtime again, and I remembered the storm I had encountered there six years previously. I left the forest supervisor's office with a smile. The canyon surrounding Big Tree, with the backdrop waterfalls would indeed be a great place for any ceremony, and especially for a wedding.

On the day of the event, which was set for midafternoon, I hiked into the canyon early and spent the day. I packed a picnic lunch with peanut butter, my favorite staple for the field or woods, and some of my mother's canned and pickled hot peppers to spice up the sandwich. Fresh fruit added just the right final touch, and a canteen of cold cranberry juice helped put out the fire from the garden-grown peppers.

Members of the wedding party, some from as far away as Texas, began gathering shortly after lunch and by 2 p.m., I had found a rather secluded seat on a rock a safe distance away. There was a good view of the proceedings. I hadn't been settled for long on the moss-clad stone before a softspoken fellow in full tuxedo approached me and introduced himself as Charles Maples, the groom. I wished him luck, and he invited me to the wedding. It wasn't necessary, of course—I was already there, and I felt I had a right to be, since I had visited these woods years earlier. I did move a bit closer after the wedding started, however.

The bride, named Barbara, wore a long lace white dress. The bridesmaid, best man, flower girls, and minister were all dressed formally. It was impressive, to say the least. The falls in the background and the rush of water in the brook leading down to Sipsey Fork provided the music. There must have been thirty people there, all of them hiking the mile or more through the woods and climbing down those precarious cliffs to get there. It was a wedding I'll never forget.

From that day on, Barbara and Charlie Maples became special friends of mine, and we've kept in touch a good many years. Barbara even chose to study nature photography with me and sometime later attended my Everglades wildlife photography workshop. Her wedding was one of the most memorable of my lifetime—certainly in terms of setting. The old-growth forest and its memories became even more precious to me.

For several nights afterward, I camped in the wonderfully silent Sipsey along Bee Branch, which provided a gentle, bubbly music for me all through the night. Great horned owls called from the faraway chambers of the forest; close by, in the early-morning hours, were the chirps and chatters of squirrels and the songs of many birds. Black-throated and green warblers darted from tree to tree. Pileated wood-peckers drummed on hollow snags in the canyon, their sounds muffled by green moss along the canyon walls.

The Bee Branch area of the Sipsey Wilderness is undoubtedly one of the most scenic areas in all the South. The newlyweds who carried a seventeen-foot canoe through the forest and somehow eased it down the canyon walls by moonlight a few nights before the wedding knew that all along.

It seems remarkable to me in some respects to find old-growth forest remaining in the South. After the Civil War, the South was hard-pressed to rebuild and restore what had been destroyed. The economic conditions were terrible and many of the people living there were poor indeed. Many families had lost not only their homes, but members of their family. Even the aristocratic were in dire need of money. In many cases, they turned to the remaining old-growth forests to make up the deficit.

Many tracts of old growth were left alone, such as the mysterious swamps which afforded difficult or no accessibility like Four Holes, Congaree, and Woods Bay in South Carolina, the Okefenokee in Georgia, and the Big Cypress in Florida (even though major portions of the Okefenokee and Big Cypress were logged). But there were tracts in other places which were saved simply because they were there.

Just outside the city limits of Thomasville, Georgia, for instance, a city of some 25,000, approximately 600 acres of old-growth long-needle pine stand—a monument to the dedication of the Whitley family, which still owns it to this day. It's said this is the largest and finest stand of old-growth long-needle pine remaining anywhere on the planet. Located on Greenwood Plantation, which earns most of its income as a commercial quail-hunting area, the huge pines line both sides of Pine Tree Boulevard leading out of the city, with 150-foot-tall trees three feet in diameter at the base. Although the plantation is not open to the public other than for quail hunting, manager Randy Ryan speaks of how inspiring just to drive down the road through the virgin pine forest. "It is like nothing else you could ever experience in southwest Georgia," he says.

Along the upper reaches of Florida's St. John's River, which flows north instead of south, east, or west as most rivers do in the United States, is the Tosohatchee State Preserve, under the administration of the State Park system. The Tosohatchee includes some 28,000 acres of mixed swamp and sand pine country. In many of the swamps, such as the Jim Creek Swamp along the St. John's, live some of the most impressive bald cypress old growth in the southeastern United States. Charlie Matthews, manager of the property, says some of the big trees are a good five feet in diameter at head height above the buttress.

Mississippi and Louisiana hold the greatest number of tracts of old growth in the South. Louisiana has a seventy-six-acre old-growth cypress-tupelo swamp in the heart of its capital city, Baton Rouge. Its other old-growth forests include virgin loblolly pine in Evangeline Parish north of Turkey Creek. The other notable stand is mixed long-needle and slash pine east of Mandeville in Fontainbleau State Park. The Evangeline Parish tract experienced considerable blowdown when Hurricane Audrey hit it directly a few years back. The trees in both tracts date back two-hundred years.

Over in Mississippi, several tracts still stand, like monuments to old-growth

168

forests that might have grown at one time throughout the South. A tract of forty acres of 300-year-old sweet gum 150 feet tall and nearly five feet in diameter dwells in the Delta National Forest. Not far away in the same forest is an eighty-acre tract of predominantly green ash some 250 years old, as well as another 40 acres of overcup oak with trees forty inches across at the base.

In the Noxubee National Wildlife Refuge Wilderness Area, along the Noxube River bottoms, is some 1200 acres of cypress-sweet gum which looks to be old growth. However, a close examination might disclose a few snags and stumps from cuttings around 1850, long before the Civil War brought chaos to the South.

At New Albany, Mississippi, is a private tract of some eighty acres in what is known as the Pontotoc Ridge Hardwoods, owned by Mrs. Clifton Daniel. And over near Louisville in the east central part of the state is some virgin loblolly owned by Georgia Pacific, the timber company. The trees, which date back more than one hundred years, are the star attraction of this twenty-acre park. Shortleaf pine grows on the hilly, more elevated sections of the park, while the loblolly pine stand along the creek bottom. The tract is located near the Natchez Trace Historical Trail.

Slightly southwest of the Georgia Pacific park at the town of Forest is the Bienville Pines Scenic Area, a part of Bienville National Forest. Containing some 189 acres, it is the largest-known block of residual old-growth loblolly and shortleaf pine forest in the state. With trees dating back some 200 years, it is part of a forest also containing mixed hardwoods.

Opposite, left. *Great Egret, Tosohatchee Wilderness.*
Opposite, right. *Dead swamp gum riddled by the pecking of the pileated woodpecker Pascagoula Swamp.*
Above. *Throughout the South are old-growth live oaks, some of which are hundreds of years old, such as this one dating back 1500 years on Cumberland Island, Georgia.*

Sandbar, Pascagoula River, Mississippi.

Bald cypress in the Pascagoula Swamp.

Bald Cypress.

The Bienville Pines forest owes its existence to the Bienville Lumber Company, which owned the land for many years before its purchase by the U.S. Forest Service in 1935. The company had saved it because the town of Forest expressed interest in it as a potential town park. It was located close to the sawmill and railroad shipping point, so the lumber company could easily hold onto it. It was handy, and could be cut at any time they chose. They didn't, and the result is an impressive old-growth forest that is home to the endangered red cockaded woodpecker, pileated woodpeckers, wild turkey, squirrel, raccoon, and fox. Some sightings of bobcat have been reported.

To the extreme southeast down on the Gulf Coast is the Pascagoula Swamp, which lies along the singing river. For ages, the Pascagoula River has been known as the "singing river" because of a low humming sound it makes. Indian legend has it these are the sounds of their ancestors who were drowned in the river. Close along the banks of the Pascagoula is a mixed old-growth cypress and tupelo gum swamp covering several hundred acres. Now owned by the state of Mississippi and operated as a preserve, it is one of the finest examples of river swamp in the state.

It was late March the first time I visited the Pascagoula. I was there on assignment for *Oceans* magazine to do an article on swamps like the Pascagoula that favorably affected the oceans. The first few days were cold and cloudy. Winter still hung on precariously even though the calendar said it was spring. Gradually, however, the afternoons became sunny and warmer until, by the time I departed, it was beginning to feel springlike. The cold had put a hold on the mosquitoes, however, and the stay was most pleasant. I really didn't want to leave.

Pools left by the flooding winter river provided mirrors for the giant trees. Bald cypress and gum grew profusely throughout the swamp and, this early in the year, there was virtually no understory or vegetation growing on the floor of the forest. Only small clumps of weedy vegetation and wildflowers had awakened to the early call of the sun.

All across the South trees do well if left alone by humankind, simply because there almost always is an abundance of water. While drought periods do occur, they are infrequent. Even the air, with humidity levels reaching upwards of 90 percent much of the time for about six months of the year, helps to give trees the moisture they need for growth. Daily rainfall occurs during the summer months in many geographical locations. In other words, as one old Georgia cracker put it, "It's sweatin' weather."

It wasn't yet "sweatin' weather" in the Pascagoula in April, but in another month it would be both hot, muggy, and buggy. "Mosquitoes big as Cessnas," one resident of the area told me. "They'll durn near carry you off."

There are dry places in this swamp, but not many, and not at this time of year, either. The ground was sopping wet even aside from the pools. Winter rains sometimes swell the river to overflow, which then feeds the swamp. The swamp gum and bald cypress can pull as much as a ton of water from the ground per tree during hot summer days when high rates of transpiration occurs. All this moisture being fed into the air by trees is what caused President Reagan to utter his infamous statement that trees were one of the chief polluters, surpassing even automobiles. He was wrong, of course, but his words would long be remembered by nature lovers everywhere.

The Pascagoula River, Mississippi.

Deep inside the Pascagoula tract were trees more than 200 years old, some 150 feet tall, and four feet through near the base. Some of the old cypress, which have bellowed buttresses, exceed even that in diameter. As soon as the days warmed even a little bit, the downed logs and cypress knees would become places where cottonmouth moccasins and other water snakes would emerge from the murky waters to sun. Throughout the South, particularly where there is standing water, poisonous cottonmouths live. Other poisonous snakes are also found in many southern old-growth woodlands—pygmy rattlers, which rarely are more than a foot to eighteen inches long; copperheads, which are also small but may reach two feet to thirty inches; and the eastern timber rattler, which sometimes climbs trees and shrubs and can reach a length of five feet. Closer to the coastal lowlands forest, great diamondback rattlers are sometimes found. A fellow in southeast Georgia once showed me a local newspaper photo of one that had been shot that was over six feet long and weighed eighty-nine pounds.

While I was working on *The Island* on an island off the coast of Georgia, I came across one old rattler (not in an old-growth forest, but in sparse woodlands) which I would estimate at over fifty pounds. It was the largest snake I had ever seen outside of a zoo. There was, needless to say, no confrontation. I turned and made my way carefully and cautiously back the way I had come. Later, when I worked in the upper Amazon rainforest, I was reminded of that great rattler as I listened to stories from the native Indians about the bushmaster, said to be the world's largest toxic snake. As large as my Georgia rattler? I never got to find out.

Old rattlers and old growth . . . I have a high degree of respect for both. But I'll pass on any more old rattlers, thank you.

ELEVEN

The Forest and the City

You can find many exciting things in cities, but something you would not expect to find is an ancient forest. Yet they somehow miraculously do exist. In such unlikely places as Indianapolis, New London, Connecticut, Baton Rouge, San Francisco, and even Washington, D.C., stand forests made up of trees 200 to 300 or more years old. If you considered single, scattered old trees dating back two or three centuries, then a good many more cities could be added to the list.

Let's face it. We all, every one of us, like trees. I firmly believe there's not a timber baron anywhere, for instance, that couldn't be counted in the ranks of tree lovers. Ask any one of them if they'd rather see a world without trees and they would surely answer an emphatic no. A world without trees would be intolerable.

It is largely because of this love affair and unusual respect for trees that such tracts either within or in close proximity to cities and towns survived urban sprawl. In the small town of Tomahawk, Wisconsin, for instance, it was the Bradley family's love of trees that gave the town one of the most outstanding parks in America—Bradley Woods. For several generations the Bradley family, which had industrial interests in the neighborhood, protected the park (then called Hogsback Park) until after patriarch Bill Bradley's death in 1903.

In 1920, the officers of the Bradley Corporation sold the park to the city of Tomahawk for just $10,000. It included 125 acres of fine old-growth red pine, some of them dating back 250 years. There was also white pine, old oak, and maple. They are all still there, but the red pines began declining some years ago from overuse and abuse by campers and picnickers. Camping finally was stopped in 1976, although foresters say it may have been too late. Still, it stands today as a fine living monument of a bygone era in that part of central Wisconsin.

Overleaf *Muir Woods, near San Francisco, California.*

Among other old-growth forests in urban areas about the country is one in greater Washington, D.C., which narrowly escaped the chainsaw. In fact, a good portion of it didn't. In 1979, while working on a nature guidebook to Washington, D.C., I discovered a fine tract of mixed mesophytic forest just north of the Washington Beltway in Maryland. It was called Belt Woods. Later I learned it was owned by the Episcopal Church, which was looking to sell it. The handwriting was on the wall, and I figured it would only be a matter of time before the land would be stripped of its huge trees.

Shortly thereafter I was in the office of Ray Culter, who was then in charge of Protection Projects with The Nature Conservancy in Arlington, Virginia. I spoke to Ray about it. "We weren't aware of any old-growth forest in greater Washington," he told me. They looked into the possibility of purchasing the tract and offering some sort of protection. The church was not interested in selling, and some five or six years later, logging began.

Meanwhile, the state of Maryland stepped in and purchased some 109 acres of the forest. They promptly set them aside as a state park preserve, but did not encourage public attendance. It does have the name, however, of Belt Woods State Park, and it includes only some fifty acres of old growth—great oak, northern and southern yellow poplar, and hickory, some of them five feet in diameter and 150 feet tall. Other trees are scarlet oak, black oak, black gum, black cherry, and, in the understory, dogwood, spicebush, sweet haw, ironwood, and mockernut hickory. Pawpaw, holly, American elm, and redbud are also there. On the forest floor are May apple, bloodroot, snakeroot, wild yam, showy orchid, cranefly orchid, rattlesnake fern, Indian pipe, Christmas fern, and Solomon seal.

In 1974, the Secretary of the Interior designated the south tract of Belt Woods as a National Natural Landmark, which set quality standards but did not provide protection.

The Society of American Foresters, a professional organization of foresters and scientists, took an interest in the woods, but finally decided they could only afford to be serious about the south tract. But they couldn't even raise the money for that.

The farm on which the woods stands was operated by W. Seton Belt for many years. He died in the late 1950s, and in his will named the Episcopal Diocese of Washington as benefactor. He specified, however, that the trustee "shall in general keep the land fertile and productive, provided, however, that the timber on said farm shall not be sold but shall only be used for the purpose of repairs and improvements to the buildings and fences and for firewood... my home shall be used as a retirement home for Episcopal clergy, or for some other suitable purposes..."

It was clear Belt intended the forest to be protected, but loosely worded phrases such as the clause "or for some other suitable purposes" or "shall use its best judgment as it sees fit" provided the option for the trustee to log the forest.

"It is as magnificent a forest as you'll ever see anywhere in the eastern states north of the Smokies," says Daniel Boone, a forest ecologist with The Wilderness Society who lives near Belt Woods. "I go there and walk back through the woods every chance I get. It's simply a religious experience to get back into the old growth— so different and so refreshing after spending a day in Washington."

Boone, who claims he's no relation to the legendary namesake, has been working with the church to try to maintain forest corridors in adjacent parts of the property, which in 1992 were scheduled for housing development. "It would help immensely if we could have the church maintain some adjacent lands as old-growth forest."

Not far away, at the U.S. Fish & Wildlife Service's Patuxent Research Station, is a seven-acre island, part of a 2670-acre preserve. A fine stand of huge old beech trees said to be nearly 250 years old lives there. I went there a few years ago to see them, wading a shallow portion of the river in August to get onto the island. Since the research center is closed to the public, the grounds on which the beech grow are fairly well-protected. In fact, a good many members of the staff at the research center don't even know about these big beech trees. They are very impressive.

Up the coast in New England, which hardly has any old growth at all to brag about, are the remains of a seventy-acre hemlock stand at the Connecticut College Arboretum in the city of New London. While a great deal of damage was done to this forest by a hurricane which swept up from the Caribbean in 1938, there still are impressive old trees at least 400 years old.

Down in Georgia, which happens to be the largest state east of the Mississippi River, are several noteworthy tracts of old-growth forest, one of them actually within the city limits of Atlanta. Called Fernbank, this sixty-five-acre preserve has trees standing 200 feet tall and 300 years old—shortleaf and loblolly pine, northern red oak, and pignut hickory. Many of them were already old when General Sherman burned Atlanta and began his fiery march to the sea during the Civil War.

Fernbank is thought to be the largest old-growth forest in a suburban location in the entire Piedmont region of the United States; it has never been logged and was fenced for protection years ago by farsighted conservationists. Today it is leased by the DeKalb County school system as a study forest. It has suffered in other ways, however. In the mid-1970s, for instance, armies of southern pine beetles swept through Georgia and killed more than 400 big pines there. But it is still a remarkable forest, particularly in view of its location in the largest city of the southeastern United States.

Directly to the north on the doorstep of Rome, Georgia, is Marshall Woods, owned by The Nature Conservancy. To the southwest at Thomasville, Georgia, is privately owned Greenwood Plantation (described in Chapter 11). Marshall Woods, located within the city limits of Rome, lies adjacent to the Coosa River. It was purchased in 1880 by the Marshall family, who set about preserving the woodlands for posterity. In 1976, Maclean Marshall gave the land to The Nature Conservancy shortly before his death. That group, along with an organization called Friends of Marshall Forest, now manages it as a forest preserve. It contains some 250 acres, of which one hundred acres is old-growth forest.

Marshall Woods has some 300 species of plants on the property, some of which are trees. At least five species of plantlife found here is considered rare in Georgia, including one on the list of nationally endangered species. The predominant tree species are loblolly and shortleaf pine, with a mixture of hardwoods such as white oak, northern red oak, and magnolia.

To the west in Louisiana are two city swamp forests—one on the campus of Southwest Louisiana State University at Lafayette and the other in Baton Rouge. The

179

Right. *Giant beech trees in the Patuxent Research Station, Maryland.*
Below left. *Loblolly pine in the Marshall Woods are more than 200 years old.*
Below right. *Marshall Woods, in Rome, Georgia, now belongs to The Nature Conservancy.*

one located on-campus used to be a hog pen, believe it or not, but the old-growth cypress suited the hogs a lot better than the hogs suited them. The trees survived, however, and today give the campus a big cypress sanctuary in its midst.

In the state's capital city, Baton Rouge, is Bluebonnet Swamp, with seventy-six acres of old-growth cypress and tupelo trees. The forest is privately owned in three parts—two roughly equal areas divided between Dr. and Mrs. Hans Armstrong and the Staring and Knox families, and the third comprising some five acres owned by the Louisiana Savings Association. All three landowners have preserved the forest in its primitive setting.

Yankeeland, Indianapolis, maintains a city park that contains some of the largest old-growth forest in Indiana. The park, located on College Avenue, was preserved for years by the Marott family and now carries the Marott name. It was given to the city by George Marott in memory of his wife for "the enjoyment of nature." Although it contains only nineteen acres of natural ravine land, it has a mixed old-growth forest of shagbark hickory, white oak, red oak, tulip poplar, and sycamore. Some of the trees are four to five feet in diameter. The park is close by the White River, which flows through the city, and contains a total of eighty-three acres, the remainder in second-growth woods and open meadows.

The ultimate in old-growth forests in urban areas, however, is epitomized by Muir Woods of San Francisco (just over the Golden Gate). The Woods are composed mainly of redwoods and are named after conservationist John Muir. With its huge redwoods eight to ten feet in diameter and more than 250 feet tall, it stands as a perfect monument to the memory of the man who was the founder and first president of the Sierra Club.

One of the people Muir inspired to contribute to the embryonic conservation movement in the late 1800s was Congressman William Kent of Marin County. The congressman purchased 500 acres of threatened redwood forest in 1908 and petitioned President Teddy Roosevelt to designate it a national monument. Roosevelt agreed, and established safe protection for this magnificent forest, which is still operated as a park open to the public.

Muir Woods are also a haven for wildlife such as blacktail deer, varied birdlife, and all kinds of small animals. During winter Redwood Creek is a spawning stream for silver salmon and steelhead trout.

Perhaps the old-growth urban forests are the most endangered of all, at least in one respect. They suffer from several symptoms far more severely than isolated old-growth forests far away from cities. The greatest impact is made by people who love the forest; they trample it to death, compacting the soil, spreading litter, chipping the bark off the trees, or carving their initials and messages on them. In the course of doing field work for this book, I walked many a trail, and in some cases found my own path where no others had recently walked. I found initials, some of them a hundred years or more old, carved in the tree bark everywhere. If it does not harm the trees—and it does, if only to a small degree—it certainly disturbs the aesthetics of an old-growth forest.

Secondly, pollution is by far greater in urban forests than in those far removed—everything from groundwaters filtered through landfill dumps to air filled with contaminants from factories, fumes from automobile exhausts, and even heavy metals from sewage treatment plants. The fish that spawn within the Olympic Rainforest come there from the Pacific Ocean, and just thirty-eight miles out on the north end of the Farallon Islands is a nuclear waste dump. Does this now or will it in the future have some effect either directly or indirectly on the park, or upon the great trees that grow there? Scientists and political leaders emphatically say no. But haven't similar denials preceded some very serious environmental tragedies?

We must keep our fingers crossed for all old-growth forests everywhere, and for their longevity, but we should be particularly concerned about the urban forests. Tomahawk, Wisconsin, with a population of less than 5000, claims the purest water in the world with twenty-five natural lakes and four rivers flowing within a radius of twenty-five miles. It's too bad they can't share their good water and clean air with other urban old growths throughout the nation.

Opposite. *The towering redwoods of Muir Woods.*

TWELVE

To Kill a Forest

For many years the best way to kill a forest was to employ some very simple methods—a match, a saw, an ax. With those three tools, man succeeded in destroying virtually all the old-growth forest that covered vast areas of America. In doing so, he was able to create cultivatable farm land for growing grains and hay crops and grazing animals. Later, some of this farm land would be sacrificed to urban sprawl. Without those simple tools, this nation would, quite frankly, never have become the world power and leader it did as a result of the Industrial Revolution. The forest for many years has played a significant role in the development of this country. It still does, and likely will for many years to come.

For ages, vast forests covered the continent from the Atlantic Ocean to the Mississippi Valley and from the Rockies westward. They offered an inexhaustible supply of wood for building houses and for keeping them warm. Yet for a time the forest slowed the movement of pioneers westward. It concealed wild animals such as bear, cougar, and wolves, as well as the Native American—all of whom threatened the new settlers. "The pioneer," said frontier historian Frederick Jackson Turner, "must wage a hand-to-hand combat against the forest, cutting and burning a little space to let in the light upon a dozen acres of hard-won soil."

From the beginning of our nation's history, we have indeed looked upon wilderness as something to be conquered. The sooner the forest could be cleared, the better. It was an obstacle to be overcome at whatever expense, so the land could be converted to something more economically productive. After World War II, that meant housing subdivisions and industrial parks. We created more jobs, and more people could afford to buy houses—most of them built of wood products which required more cutting of trees. The process accelerated, and few people concerned themselves with the fact that all the big trees were being cut.

Opposite. *Not only are many foresters practicing clearcutting, but they burn what's left on the spot, thus creating an erosion problem in heavy-rain climates.*

185

Timber companies and the U.S. Forest Service kept assuring the public that trees were a renewable resource. According to them, sources of lumber would never run out. But everyone knew, if they possessed any reasoning power at all, that our population was expanding by enormous rates and as long as we were able to maintain a healthy economy, there would be strong demand for more and more timber.

We have an insatiable appetite for the forest. In order to keep the economy afloat, Washington claims we must keep building, and they hope for another thirty million new homes over the next couple of years. That will eat up billions of acres of forest. Each Sunday, *The New York Times*, weighing about eight pounds per newspaper, consumes about 175 acres of trees. Dairy Queen, Kentucky Fried Chicken, and McDonald's gorge themselves on our forests. McDonald's alone chews up some 315 square miles of woods every year for paper cups, napkins, wrapping paper, sacks, and straws.

We are a nation of waste. Much could be recycled, and much of our wasteful ways could be rethought. We are beginning to, but we are fifty years too late. We need to teach our children to be better than we are. Think of how many trees are tossed out as litter along the roadside, or dumped in landfills across America to create still more problems. The bottom line is that it's killing the American forests. It is the responsibility of every man, woman, and child alive to do something about it.

Meanwhile, the monster still rampages on. Not only have we sought to devour the last remaining old growth in America, we have now attacked the Amazon rainforest. I've been told that timber interests, in order to keep up with insatiable demands, clearcut an area the size of Indiana every year. I believe it, because I have flown over some of those regions where clearcutting is occurring. Once in Ecuador, I sat next to a timber executive from Arkansas on a commuter airliner bucking its way across the Andes from the rainforest. After he described some of his company's operations to me, I asked him how they dealt with the native Indians in the rainforest, many of whom are quite primitive.

"Well," he said, showing some exasperation. "They're proving much more difficult than we imagined. We thought by encouraging religious orders in the United States to send in missionaries the problem would be solved. They could teach them Christianity and perhaps some English and make them understand the white man's ways and how that could bring them a much improved lifestyle. But many of the Indians have resisted that. In fact, a couple of years ago, they rounded up and killed a bunch of missionaries. We may have to find some new way to deal with this problem."

How ironic, I thought to myself. We have employed God to help destroy the Amazon rainforest.

As a result of human demand, irresponsible timber interests have left entire clearcut forests looking like the WWII Dresden firebombing. The rainforest in the Amazon Valley of Brazil, along with its complex ecosystem, is significantly damaged, perhaps so much that in time the whole of this hemisphere's environment will be adversely affected. Forest researcher Erik Eckholm of the United Nations says it also could cause the extinction of thousands of plant and animal species, and it might even change the global climate. In southern California's San Bernardino National

One of the quickest and most devastating destroyers of a whole forest landscape in recent times was the Mt. St. Helens eruption of May 1980. This stand of trees extended for hundreds of square miles around the volcano, but within seconds, every tree was felled like a matchstick.

Forest, air pollution—specifically, ozone damage and acid rain caused by the burning of fossil fuels—is killing off pines. Scientists are keeping a close watch on the redwoods and sequoias, the largest trees on earth, for indications that manmade pollution is having some critical effect upon them. Half the red pine in New England above 2500 feet, which flourished as late as the sixties, are dead today. In the Piedmont and mountain regions of the Southeast, the rate at which yellow pines died increased 60 percent from 1975 to 1985.

Fires, of course, are very damaging to forests that cannot tolerate fire. The hardwoods do not like that much heat and many hardwood trees die from a single forest fire. On the other hand, many trees are almost immune to fire; some even like it. The giant sequoias and redwoods have a high tolerance for fire, simply because of the thickness of their armorlike bark. The fires in Yellowstone National Park in 1988, which consumed almost a million acres, were assumed to have caused devastating damage. They actually did little or no ecological damage and may even have done some good. Lodgepole pines provided most of the fuel for the fires, but some lodgepole pine cones are serotinous, opening and releasing seeds only in a fire's heat.

Upon several working assignments in the Pacific Northwest during the 1970s and 1980s, I personally became much concerned with the clearcutting I saw and the hauling away of great numbers of big trees. The millyards I passed in Oregon and Washington were all filled with enormous piles of huge logs waiting to be converted

Eventually ocean storms topple the old trees and currents carry them away—either deposited on another shore or caught in ocean rivers such as the Gulf Stream and carried across the sea. This one is in South Carolina.

into timber products of one sort or another. The vegetation of the mountains and river valleys was disappearing before my very eyes as small armies of men with chain saws marched on the forest. The devastation was disgusting to the eye. It was that sight that convinced me that in no time at all most of the big trees would be cut and there would be no forests left.

In 1978, I began talking to older employees of the U.S. Forest Service in Washington and Oregon about the demise of the old growth. Most of them seemed unconcerned, but finally I met a forester in Shelton on Puget Sound who was honest and open with his opinions. Having spent twenty years in the U.S. Forest Service, most of it in the Pacific Northwest, he candidly admitted to me that he figured (and so did the Forest Service, he said) there was only about ten years left before all the big trees would be cut on Forest Service property. After that, they would be forced to turn to second and third growth.

"And what is this going to do for the timber industry?" I asked. "Lumber quality will become lower and lower," he said. "Eventually, in my opinion, sometime soon we'll come to a point where lumber products as we know them will cease to be—we'll only have timber products like particle board and chipboard with which to build."

Upon returning home to the Midwest, where I then lived, I wrote a long letter to the late Senator Henry (Scoop) Jackson. I had come to admire him over the years not only for some of his environmental stands in Congress, but because of his own personal background. We corresponded frequently until he died; at one time, when he announced his candidacy for the Presidency, I felt we might have some chance of saving the forest. But that didn't last long, of course.

Upon more than one occasion during the 1970s I noticed increasing Japanese activity in the forests of the Pacific Northwest. Sometimes they logged selectively with balloons so they could take out the big trees without disturbing others. If big trees were to be cut, I thought, this is better than clearcutting. But I disliked the idea that foreign corporations were permitted to cut big trees in our country and take them away. Since the old growth was severely limited, I felt that what cutting did occur ought to be used to supply the needs of Americans.

I was told by Senator Jackson at the time that no cutting for exportation could occur on public lands, but that there were no laws on the books to prevent private U.S. companies such as Weyerhaeuser from bidding on contracts within the national forests and using those cuttings for domestic use. Those same corporations could then cut trees from private lands for export to Japan and other places. The result, in my mind, was one and the same. The bottom line was that the old-growth forests were steadily being diminished and by the end of the nineties would all be gone, except for portions set aside in the national parks.

The main market for American timber then was Japan which, in the midst of a tremendous housing boom, began offering twice what American mills would pay for old-growth trees. The American timber companies could only see dollar signs and not only shipped the Japanese the raw logs, but with them American jobs. The Japanese took all they could get, stockpiling them until, as one U.S. Congressman from Oregon put it, "the docks at the Japanese mills were piled high as Mount Fuji."

For some time in 1989 Weyerhaeuser had to shut down some of its logging operations because the docks were full of logs on both sides of the Pacific. But it didn't last long. The Japanese realized a good thing when they saw it and gobbled up everything they could. They even stationed lumber milling ships just outside the three-mile boundary limits in the Pacific Northwest and processed timber at sea, then sold it back to the Americans.

If our wilderness areas and national parks were opened for grabs, it would take the timber barons only months to strip them of every last tree. As one environmentalist put it, "I think they're looking for that last old-growth tree and I'd almost bet odds-on that they'd fight over who had the honors—if we could consider it an honor—of cutting it down." Oregon environmentalist Lou Gould calls it "the last great buffalo hunt."

Fire is another killer of trees, although some trees benefit by it because they need the heat of fire to help with reseeding.

When a moratorium was put on timber cutting on public lands in the Pacific Northwest's northern spotted owl habitat area, the lumbermen were furious. Some of them organized hunts for the owl—to shoot it down. Even though it had been placed on the endangered species list by the U.S. Fish and Wildlife Service, the owl meant nothing but trouble for the loggers. Loggers' cafes added "owl stew" to their menus. In Forks, Washington, logging suspenders emblazoned with "Spotted Owl Hunter" became fashionable.

Even now, we cannot take for granted that the trees are fully protected. Poaching of the big western cedars is a constant problem in protected old-growth forests. Several years ago I learned that poachers were using large helicopters at night to lift the big trees right out of the Olympic National Park. And upon more than one occasion, whenever sufficient reasons arose, the big trees have been threatened. President Wilson even cut the size of the Olympic National Park during World War I so sitka spruce old growth could be harvested to build airplanes. In those days, lightweight wood was used in the framework construction of airplanes. (Remember Howard Hughes's Spruce Goose of World War II vintage, which even today is a tourist attraction at Long Beach, California?) The harvest of forests growing within the park never occurred because the war ended before lumberjacks got there. But it makes one leery, to say the least, that old-growth forests, and our national parks as well, always stand in jeopardy, should the need arise to invade them for their natural resources. Had Hughes's plan for building huge planes of lightweight spruce, for instance, been implemented during World War II, there likely would have been

Front-end-loader machinery is brought in occasionally to clean the land and stack debris for burning after a cleanout.

serious threats to the old-growth forest inside and outside the national parks of the Pacific Northwest and Alaska.

Recently the Pacific yew, a small tree quite often found among old-growth forest stands, has been found to contain an ingredient which may provide a cure for breast cancer. Since that discovery, the Pacific yew has been eagerly sought by drug companies and the National Cancer Institute. The drug, taxol, is found in the bark of the yew. The yew, sometimes considered more an understory shrub than a tree and insignificant otherwise, was being killed out by old-growth cutting which exposed it to too much damaging heat and light.

The threats to the yew and several other species of wildlife which cannot survive without old growth has led to greater attention and emphasis upon biodiversity. It is a concept being discussed more and more in the halls of various research universities as well as the U.S. Government. In fact, Congressman Gerry Studds of Massachusetts, who is promoting its cause in Congress, calls biodiversity "a fancy way of saying that it takes all kinds to make a world." That world is more diverse than we've ever been led to believe in the past, with only about 60 percent of the nation's 250,000 species identified at this point. If we haven't identified them, how can we know their importance to the ecosystem or what they may contribute toward solving some of the problems known to man? Everything in nature is inter-related. Nothing stands alone, and if we eliminate one factor, we disturb and run the risk of destroying countless other factors.

The elimination of old-growth forest not only takes away the ancient big trees, but we now know it also destroys other things as well. That fact was illustrated in the Pacific Northwest in the late 1980s when it was found that the little spotted owl will likely be eliminated from the planet with the cutting of old-growth forest. The endangered owl is an indicator species, and its dwindling numbers signal the decline of the Northwest's ancient forest ecosystem as well as the many species that it comprises.

The northern spotted owl weighs in at less than two pounds. It is about seventeen inches tall and is packaged in white-barred brown feathers. Insofar as we know, it has little status—a shy bird, nothing like the American bald eagle—except that it is, like all life forms, important in the chain of life. Researchers still have a lot to learn about them: it was just discovered in the 1980s that they only nest in rotting snags of old-growth forest. Without a suitable nesting habitat, they cannot survive. Researchers used tiny radio transmitters on selected birds to plot their subsistence range. Earlier estimates had been around 300 acres for a pair of nesting owls. Then improved research broadened the range to 2000 acres. The new findings began to concern members of the U.S. Forest Service, and in the late 1980s, old-growth cutting on most public lands in the Pacific Northwest was shut down. Canada did likewise in areas known to be inhabited by the northern spotted owl. The furor raised by timbermen was loud, and little lumber towns like Forks, Washington, began to close down. Residents started moving away because they had no jobs and no hopes of any. But they still refused to admit there was any problem with cutting old growth, as though the ancient forests would go on and on forever.

One recent July day, I flew with Dan Sullivan, a Forks timberman who owned his own plane, over some of the Olympic Rainforest area. Outside the national park, vast stretches of clear cut acreage spread out under us. It was far greater than I had anticipated and I mentioned my concerns to Dan. "Looks like just about everything has been cut," I lamented. But he was not worried. "Oh, there's lots of good timber down there yet," he answered. "Be a long, long time before we ever run out. Besides, it grows so fast. In twenty years all that clearcut down there will be covered with trees well on their way to market size."

I felt a great sadness. Not at Dan's answer, but at the mere idea of all that marvelous green turned black and brown and bare. And no matter the contention of lumbermen, the old growth would never be again. Once cut, it was gone forever. We can never replace trees 2000 years old. The mere thought of it was sickening. The primeval forest, here in one of America's final strongholds, had shrunk to almost nothing.

Whenever I visited the Olympic Peninsula in the 1960s and 1970s I braced myself for driving in logging-truck traffic on crooked U.S. 101, which circled the peninsula. It was like dealing with an Army convoy. The trucks were virtually taking both sides of the road, as quota drivers sped their rigs at breakneck speed to get in as many loads a day as possible. Most carried seven or eight logs on their long trailers; occasionally I saw trucks with only three logs and marveled at the size of the felled giants.

During those same visits, I would occasionally see old black-and-white photographs taken earlier in this century of trucks hauling just one huge log. That was all they could get on the truck. I was sure I would never see the likes of that during my

Above. *Logging mill, Washington.*
Right. *Scotch broom, a plant
introduced along the highways of
Washington, scatters like wildfire
into deforested areas such as this
one near Forks. It is an exotic
plant that tends to crowd out other
plants and trees.*

Right. *Five years before this photograph was taken on Washington's Olympic Peninsula, a fine forest ecosystem was annihilated. The forest will replace itself in another 500 years, but in the meantime literally millions of dependent communities of life have not only been disturbed but in many cases wiped out entirely.*

Below. *The U.S. Forest Service spends taxpayer money to construct hundreds of miles of road into the forest to facilitate the removal of lumber. Logging trucks on such roads aggravate erosion problems.*

lifetime, but I was wrong. After the spotted owl controversy began, but before public lands were closed to old-growth logging, I saw many trucks on the highway with just one log. It was obvious that the timber companies, furtive in their efforts to grab everything they could as quickly as possible, were again cutting old-growth trees so huge a semi-truck could only carry one log.

Going farther north does not help. The same problems that exist in Washington's Olympic Peninsula also exist in Alaska. So much clearcutting has been done in some areas of southeast Alaska and Western Canada that fishermen in the villages there say that the erosion is simply ruining the fishing. In Kyuquot, British Columbia, villagers say there's so much silt on the bottom of the ocean that their traps set for prawns are literally covered up. The same problem with erosion exists in Alaska. I recently learned that the U.S. Forest Service had been getting as little as two dollars a tree—operating at a terrible loss and subsidizing the timber industry by building roads into timber sales areas. Since 1980, the Forest Service has lost more than $350 million of the taxpayers' money on sales of timber from just the Tongass National Forest in Alaska.

The story of old-growth forest depletion continues in other parts of the nation. As recently as 1986, the U.S. Forest Service opened portions of the Sequoia National Forest in California to timber cutting. While there were no old-growth sequoia cut at that time, the cutting of sequoias 200 to 300 years of age as well as numerous other species among the museum-stature trees was allowed. Eliminating these trees opened up the forest to potential windfall danger among the giant trees, but the Forest Service seemed unconcerned.

Were it not for the alertness of two environmentalists—Charlene Little and Carla Cloer, who discovered the cutting in August of 1986—the logging among important groves of old-growth sequoias might still be going on. It was not until the summer of 1989, however, after seventeen months of negotiations, that the cutting was brought to a halt.

In 1991, the Forest Service announced plans to log old-growth Ponderosa pine from the Fremont National Forest in Oregon—trees that were already huge before Columbus set sail toward America. They're doing this despite the opinion of some of their own research scientists that this area is unique and too scientifically valuable to be destroyed.

What many organizations and timber corporations fail to realize—or at least recognize—is that not only are they destroying the remaining old growth, but that there also is an entire system, well-balanced according to nature's laws, that is violently disrupted with the cutting of the big trees. That is particularly true of clearcutting, of course, where the ground is virtually swept clean of all living plant life, but it is even true of selective cutting. To disturb the delicate balance nature has worked out over eons of time is probably far more critical than is the loss of the big trees.

Maybe it would be easier to deal with the cutting of cathedral old growth trees if we took a serious look at history. The ancient Druids actually worshipped trees. In his classic book on myth and religion, *The Golden Bough,* Sir James Frazer recounts that ancient Greeks, Swedes, and Slavs were all tree-worshippers. According to their beliefs, the health of the trees was intimately bound to the life of the human spirit.

The Germans had a way of dealing with it—and far more sternly, too. According to Frazer, in old German law the punishment for just peeling the bark of a tree was to extract the perpetrator's navel with a sharp knife and nail it to the tree's injured area; then "he was to be drawn round and round the tree till his guts were wound about its trunk." Perhaps Frazer should be required reading for every clearcutter in the country.

Jerry Franklin of the University of Washington has done extensive research on old growth as an ecosystem. He has served as a consultant to the U.S. Forest Service, and in that capacity has spent some thirty-plus years on field research, including the monitoring of new woody plant life in the Mt. St. Helens volcanic eruption area. He has also done studies on nurse logs in the rainforest, and probably is one of America's most noted authorities on old-growth forest. Franklin vehemently abhores clearcutting.

"There should never be a clearcut," says Franklin. "Some old trees, snags, and logs should remain for continuity of dependent communities. If you want life to survive, you have to build a bridge."

That thought is shared by Chris Maser, who worked for years with the Bureau of Land Management and the U.S. Forest Service. Today, Maser lectures and writes books on reverence for nature's methods. "We're in trouble as soon as we focus on our own limited goals and lose the broader view," he says. "When we destroy all our ancient forests, we will have thrown away nature's blueprint. We must have that blueprint if we are to save forests for the future."

One school of thought believes that it may already be too late. One theorist declares: "Somewhere out there is a single tree that will take us over the edge. Not that any single tree is that important. But it is representative of the number of old-growth trees cut, and when that one falls, added to all the rest that already have been cut, it will signal the point from which there is no return. After that, it will be impossible to restore the delicate balance of nature that insures survival of the entire ecological system."

We may have already cut that tree . . . or we may be a hundred trees past it. Who knows?

Bill Thomas, besides being a writer and pho-tographer, also gives public lectures and, since 1978, founded and directs Touch of Success Nature Photo Seminars, several of which are conducted in forests in several geographical environments. For further infor-mation on these, contact Thomas at Box 194, Lowell, Florida 32663.